Papa and Ashley

and

It's a Relationship

Papa God and Ashley

It's a Relationship

ASHLEY SCHROEDER

REDEMPTION
PRESS

Published by Redemption Press, PO Box 427, Enumclaw, WA 98022

Toll Free (844) 2REDEEM (273-3336)

Redemption Press is honored to present this title in partnership with the author. The views expressed or implied in this work are those of the author. Redemption Press provides our imprint seal representing design excellence, creative content, and high quality production.

ISBN 13: 978-1-68314-423-6 (Paperback)
978-1-68314-424-3 (Hard Cover)
978-1-68314-424-3 (ePub)
978-1-68314-426-7 (Mobi)

Library of Congress Catalog Card Number: 2017949914

Let's change the world!

Whoever humbles himself like this child
is the greatest in the kingdom of heaven.
Matthew 18:4 ESV

Victoria,

Wow! What an amazing journey.
Thank you for being apart of this
story. I am truly blessed that
you are apart of it.

Big hugs,

Ashley Schroeder

Dedication

Thank you, Papa God, for entrusting me with these encounters with You so that I can share You with others who want to know You on a deeper level through Jesus Christ my Lord and Savior.

I also dedicate this book to a group of people who are very important to me.

First are my parents. Thank you for loving me through all of life's ups and downs and for teaching me the Word of God. The best gift you have ever given me is the gift of knowing our Lord and Savior, Jesus Christ. Hey, Dad! Thanks for being like the father waiting on the hill for me when I needed to come home to Papa God. Mom, thank you for your wonderful love for people and the exceedingly amazing gift of personality that comes from God. You are a truly talented woman, and you light up the room everywhere you go!

I also dedicate this book to my husband, Kurt, and our girls, Rachael and Reagan. My heartfelt prayer for you is that this wisdom and relationship with Papa God be passed down generation to generation. Girls, you are my joy and my heart. I am so proud of you both. Thank you, Kurt, for your love and support. You have the most giving heart, and I admire that about you. I am truly blessed that you are my husband, and I love you.

Thank you, Papa and Grandmomma Mashburn for being such wonderful grandparents. I treasure you both with all my heart.

Table of Contents

Acknowledgments xi

Biography. xiii

Endorsements. xv

Foreword: The Papa God and Ashley Story. xvii

The Lost Son 25

Ladybug Dream and Wasabi! 31

Tie Your Shoelaces 41

GPS to Final Destination Lane. 51

The Voice of God 57

To Be Born Again? 63

Is Good Good Enough? 67

Last Minute Hal. 79

Engrafted into Christ 89

The God Kind of Love 101

The Persistent Widow. 107

Test the Spirits 111

Wrongly Accused 115

The World Champion 127

Healing Belongs to You 135
Facing Difficult Conversations 145
Moses Out of the Water 151
What Is Your Promised Land? 155
He Delights in Me 159
The Valley of the Shadow of Death. 163
To Know God 169
God Wants Your Heart. 175
Dark Clouds 181
The Dance 185
Thorn in My Side. 189
The Anchor for Our Souls 199
Your Weaknesses Are Your Strengths. 203
No Trespassing on Holy Ground 209
Concrete Heart 213
Center Stage. 217
Running the Race. 223
Eloi, Eloi, Lema Sabachthani 231
Glowing in the Dark 239
Grudge or Mercy 245
Do You Trust Me? 253
Value Life. 259
God Has Tentacles? 267
The Lion of Judah 275
Total Enjoyment 281

Acknowledgments

I want to acknowledge some amazing people, the first two being Pastor Debra Kaplan with Branch of Christ Ministries and Deborah Yoerg with Crowns for Christ Ministries. These two ladies have helped shape me into the godly woman I am today. I am honored to walk beside you both into our calling for our Lord and Savior Jesus Christ. May we finish our race and hear those words, "Good and faithful servant, well done!"

To Bonita Sawyer and Victoria Oberle: You are amazing women of God who have been instrumental in kick-starting the path Papa God has called me to. Wow! What a journey!

Martha Bootle and Author Kathy Jones, thank you for your wisdom and direction in writing this book. I appreciate you both and love your hearts for Papa God and His children.

To the Crowns for Christ team, Deborah Yoerg, Nikki Robles, Sonia Diaz, Madeline Hernandez and Tina Santiago-Betancourt: I am so glad to walk beside you on this amazing journey. May God bless our paths as we step out to rise and S.O.A.R on wings like eagles! (Isa. 40:31). The gift and message from Papa God in return to these amazing women of God is this:

Still, other seed fell on good soil. It came up and yielded a crop, a hundred times more than was sown. When he said this, he called out, "Whoever has ears to hear, let them hear."

His disciples asked him what this parable meant. He said, "The knowledge of the secrets of the kingdom of God has been given to you, but to others I speak in parables, so that, 'though seeing, they may not see; though hearing, they may not understand.' This is the meaning of the parable: The seed is the word of God." (Luke 8:8–11)

Biography

Ashley Schroeder is married to the love of her life, Kurt Schroeder. Kurt and Ashley have two beautiful daughters. Ashley started out in sales in 1993 and today owns her own business.

In March of 2015, Ashley started Papa God and Ashley, teaching people how to have a relationship with God, whom Ashley calls, Papa God. Motivated by her Facebook blog, "Papa God and Ashley Devotionals" and through the dreams and visions God gives her, most of these stories were prompted by her quiet time with God in His Word.

Ashley is a motivational speaker, enthusiastic author, and advocate for abused and abandoned children for Holt International, a Christian organization dedicated to finding families for the world's orphaned and abandoned children. The Lord put it on Ashley's heart, through verses like James 1:27, to raise awareness to help these children through sponsorships that provide a healthy and loving environment, proper nutrition, education and medical care.

Ashley is a natural-born speaker with an encouraging approach on who we are to Christ and as children of the King! Ashley says, "If He is the King and He is our Creator, then that makes us royalty in the kingdom of God" (See 1 Peter 2:9.)

Her inspiring stories will help you realize who you are in Christ Jesus and know that as a son or daughter of Christ, you can overcome anything that comes against you. You will rise above who the world says you are and become a true son or daughter of the King of all kings!

Please visit www.PapaGodandAshley.com to find out more about Ashley's ministry.

To learn more about adoption and sponsorship opportunities with Holt International, please go to: www.holtinternational.org.

Endorsements

Ashley is a loyal ambassador for Holt International that serves as a bridge of hope to the orphaned and vulnerable children of the world while they wait for their forever family. In this book, she brilliantly shares the biblical challenge for choosing life for the unborn child and also shares the alternative answer for abortion. Thousands of loving couples are praying for a child to adopt, love and care for without reservation—a compelling answer and hope for those who want and need it the most.

Kris Thompson
Executive Director, Holt International Children's Services

Papa God and Ashley: It's a Relationship is a book that will warm your heart. Ashley's wisdom and encouragement through these pages will captivate your heart to go deeper in your walk with the Lord. It is a beautiful opportunity to grow closer to the One who created you. Ashley is a dynamic speaker and author who will bless you with her humility and her love for *Papa God*. Be blessed, dear reader!

Deborah Yoerg
Founder, Crowns for Christ Ministries

Papa God . . . If you want to know about developing intimacy and friendship with God, this is the book for you! Ashley takes us on a wonderful journey of the friendship, revelation, and love that she has experienced with Father God.

Debra Kaplan
Senior Pastor, Branch of Christ Church
Chaplin, Pasco County Sheriff's Department
Pastoral Counselor

FOREWORD

The Papa God and Ashley Story

The name *Papa* is endearing to me because that is what I call my mom's dad.

In 2013, I attended a women's conference. The speakers, Bonita and Victoria, asked us to spend some time talking with God, and it was suggested that if there was unforgiveness in our hearts, we were to bring it to God at that time.

I will never forget the moment when I heard God's voice in my spirit. He told me that I put my papa on a pedestal (because I do love Papa Mashburn dearly). For as far back as I can remember, Papa Mashburn was the love of my life. I recall the overwhelming excitement I had as a little girl in the car rides each summer break when we would go to Georgia to see my grandparents. We had a tradition that every time we crossed the Florida-Georgia line, we would honk our car horn in gladness. I knew in my heart that my grandparents looked forward to these summer visits as well.

To give you a little insight into my grandparents, Papa Mashburn would save coins all year to give his grandbabies when we came to see him. Even as a small child, I knew that this was an act of love, and that he also had been looking forward to the summer all year long. I like to think of these coins as little tokens of love, and that he was thinking of my sister Che' and me and longing to time to spend with us.

I recall Papa Mashburn coming home from work and telling us to get ready to jump in the car to go get ice cream and do a little shopping at the mall with his saved-up money. Oh, what great memories I have of those summers. I loved swimming in the streams with my cousins and watching local Georgia football games. Vacation Bible school was always on the list of summer activities, too. Oh yes, I must not forget about picking butter beans and getting stung by a sweat bee. That was the end of that!

My grandmomma is also one of the sweetest little ladies you would ever meet. She's petite in size and soft spoken with the cutest southern drawl. She loved to bake chocolate oatmeal cookies for us, which were some of my favorites. Oh, I can even smell them now as I write!

During my time with God at this women's retreat, He reminded me of these tokens of love from my grandparents. Although I knew God was pleased I had loved my grandparents so much, I felt in my spirit that He wanted more from me; He wanted me to view Him higher than I had before. It was a very tender moment, and I knew in my heart that He wanted to be my first love.

To help you get to know me a little better, I want to tell you why this conversation with God was so imperative for me and the journey that I was about to take with God. Although I didn't know it or understand at the time, this was the beginning of my calling and my true purpose in life. God had great plans to use me, and this retreat was just the beginning of an awe-inspiring journey with God.

Over the years, people I love have disappointed me, although I believe no one did it intentionally, and most offenses were just circumstances of life or were weapons used by the enemy to divide our family. My parents are only human just like I am, and trust me, I make all kinds of mistakes. The Lord pointed out that my parents were young when they got married, and I heard God say, "Your parents were babies having babies." They both made mistakes along the way, but God is a merciful, loving and patient parent, full of grace and compassion. And I am so grateful for the sacrifices that both of my parents made to make sure my sister and I lived a safe and good life growing up. They did the best they could do with the knowledge they had at that time. God can make beauty from ashes if we trust and allow Him to lead us as both my parents have done. (See Isa. 61:3.)

Like most people's, my story is one with many twists and turns. I had a good childhood with parents who loved me, but because my family was divided due to divorce, I switched schools many times in my elementary years and went to three high schools during my teenage years. For a teenager, that is not the best scenario, but our loving God uses all things for our good. Because of family circumstances, I lived with a family friend for three months my sophomore year, and in my senior year, I moved back to Orlando and lived with my friend Dawn and her mom, Nancy. I was eighteen at this time, and it was my decision to move in with them. Prior to that, my mom and I had moved back to Georgia, but I wasn't happy there. I was a teenager and wanted to be with the friends I grew up with. Looking back on all of that, I feel horrible for what I must have put my mom through, but I was determined, and I wanted to prove I was strong and could make it on my own. Even though I was not mature and was still in high school, I was eighteen and wanted to be an adult. The problem was, I was running, but I didn't quite know what from at that moment. I know now that I was looking for a family and a relationship with the One who calls us His own, Jesus Christ.

By the time I reached my early thirties, I had run far away from the Christian values and beliefs instilled in me as a child. Finally, I went to a Christian counselor, and the Lord had me reconcile all the hurt I held in my heart against anyone.

This healing process took approximately two years, and during that time, I also apologized for the hurts I had caused others. So as you can imagine, when the speaker at the women's retreat asked us to forgive others, I thought I was good to go!

While alone with God, I proceeded to tell Him, "I do not have anyone I want to bring up to You to forgive. I have already had conversations with anyone who caused me emotional pain." Any misunderstandings I may have had before those conversations had already been clarified and rectified. I did not realize that I was still holding onto a grudge against God for those things.

In that moment God told me, "Ashley, the only One you have not forgiven is Me." Then I could hear in my spirit that God was saying, "I want to be your number One, and I want you to view Me higher than your earthly papa." Then the Lord asked me something that touched my heart to the core. He said, "Ashley, can I be your Papa?"

I was in shock! Of course, I had not realized that my heart was hardened to God in this way, and I immediately asked God to forgive me. As tears rolled down my face, I told God, "Yes, I want You to be my Papa! Please forgive me for not realizing that I held a grudge against *You*!"

Oh, how my heart sank in that very moment. I love God with all my heart. To know I had done something to hurt my Lord was just unimaginable to me. I so desperately wanted to please Him. He knew this, but for years I would only pray or call out to God when I needed something from Him. I would put God on a shelf and say, "I'll contact You if and when I need You." Like every relationship we have, there must be regular communication between both parties involved. I believe that God has feelings just like we do. After all, we were made in His image.

The naysayers or someone who may not believe in God on this level might be thinking that's an odd thing to say and do. Please understand, these are not conversations I made up or have with myself. God is a living God. If you speak to Him, He will speak to you in return. For the naysayers, I double dare you to try it. "Ask and it will be given to you; seek and you will find; knock and the door will be opened to you" (Matt. 7:7).

That day was a turning point in my life. It was when I started writing my story and I was catapulted into a deeper relationship with God. I not only acknowledged Jesus as the Savior of my life, but on a more intimate and personal level with Him that day, Jesus became my Lord.

As you can read through my writings, I am so grateful to Jesus and all that He has brought me through. After all, it's *all* about Him and not about me.

There is no condemnation in these writings, and this is not about religion. If you call me religious, I will tell you bluntly, "No, I am not religious; I have a personal relationship with my Papa God." My goal is for you to experience God on this same level and to have your own encounters with Him to share with others—to see Him as He truly is. He so desperately wants you to know Him, not just know of Him. For years, I knew of Him more than I knew Him on a personal level. To only know of someone is not having a relationship; it's division, separation, and it creates confusion about who we are and what our purpose is in this temporary world.

I think it's important to define the word *relationship* so you can see the various levels of it. Speak the hyphenated word *relationship* out loud to really hear the true meaning.

Relationship
[ri-ley-sh*uh* n-ship]
noun
1. a connection, association, or involvement
2. connection between persons by blood or marriage
3. an emotional or other connection between people: the relationship between teachers and students

Synonyms

dependence, alliance, kinship

1. affinity, consanguinity. The relationship, kinship refers to connection with others by blood or marriage. The relationship can be applied to connection, either by birth or by marriage: *relationship to a ruling family.* Kinship generally denotes common descent and implies a more intimate connection than relationship: *the ties and obligations of kinship.1*

Notice that the word *relationship* often refers to kinship, involvement, or some sort of connection with others. The root word means "to rely on" and to bring back into restoration based on the Latin version of this word.

Friend, God did not send His Son to die on a cross so we could have a religion. Jesus died and rose again so that we could reconnect with a living God full of compassion, mercy, and justice for His beloved, His sons and daughters.

God has given me this task through these chapters to show you that you can have this same kind of relationship with Him and to walk out the purpose He has for you. He loves you that much, and so do I as a brother or sister in Christ. If you don't know Him like this, then this is your chance. God is a spirit so we must connect to Him in our spirits in prayer, reading our Bibles, and worship. I will explain more about this throughout these chapters.

I have heard many people say that they have never heard God speak to them. The Holy Spirit revealed to me that this is because these people don't spend time with God reading His Word regularly, and they rarely pray with the expectation of hearing a reply from God. My question to you is this: Do you want to know God on a personal level? If you do, then come along with me on this journey. My only requirement is for

---

1   http://www.dictionary.com/browse/relationship?s=t

you to keep an open mind and heart to what God is saying to you in this book.

Several of these writings were posted on a Facebook called, "Papa God and Ashley Devotionals" in a free and less detailed, unedited format. These stories and words of inspiration come from the time I spend with God. I know He is the inspiration behind all my stories, dreams, and visions. That is why I always sign His name with mine. If it is not from the Lord, I will never sign, "Papa God." I always pray prior to writing and ask the Holy Spirit to speak through me. The awesome part is that most of the time, I have no idea what I'm going to write before I sit down. That is why I know they are from Him. I am completely and fully surrendered to His purpose when I write. I know that these stories are not only for me. They are meant for you as well, and I am ready to share them with you.

I also want to thank the people in these stories for allowing me to use our experiences for the glory of God alone. I have written them to the best of my recollection as they have occurred.

I hope these writings stir up something in you and bring you to a closer relationship with our Creator whom I call Papa God. Spend time with Him daily, and He will show you the most amazing things. If I say something more than once, well then, good! It is meant to get deeply rooted in you. Jesus told the same stories over and over, saying them in different ways because there was a point to the story every time He told them.

Oh! One more thing before we get started: I love to give hugs. My mentor, Pastor Debra Kaplan, gives the best heartfelt hugs, and I learned that hugs are a sign of kindness and warm sincerity from one person to another. It's my way of giving you my best heartfelt wishes at the end of the writings. Let's begin!

Big hugs,
Papa God and Ashley

The Lost Son

The Prodigal Son is my favorite parable probably because I can relate to it so well. I grew up in a Christian home, and my dad is one of the most amazing pastors in the world. I know what you might be thinking, "He's your dad, so you have to say that." But I am telling you, my dad tops the cake as a pastor and as a dad. I am so grateful that God put me in my family. More than anything, I am grateful to have a relationship with my Lord Jesus Christ. I attribute most of my relationship with God to my parents. They never gave up on me and constantly prayed for me, even when I didn't know they were praying. Sometimes I felt that maybe I didn't deserve their love because of my behavior. Yet they loved me anyway even if it meant loving me at times from a distance.

There was a time in my youth that I did not feel or show respect to my parents. The reason I relate to the parable of the prodigal is that I was the prodigal son, or in my case, daughter, at one point. I ran from my family, and I ran from God. Don't get me wrong; I have always loved the Lord, but there were moments when I have to admit I wondered, "Is God really there? Does He really love and care for me?" I would sit there and think, "God who are You to me, not who You are to my dad or mom?" I was on a mission to find out on my own, but I was running down the wrong path.

When I graduated from high school, I hit the ground running in the business world. I went into sales, and I knew I was good at it. I broke all sorts of sales and performance records. As a young adult, I focused mostly on my career, my husband, and my kids. That's all I was living for. You might think, "Well that's not a bad thing, Ashley." And you're right; there is nothing wrong with making a good living and taking care of our families. After all, God blessed us with our families, but as I learned later, our careers and family should not be our only focus.

God wants to be first in our lives and for us to live life to the fullest. When He created us, His intention was not to force us to love Him or to stop us from having fun. Through various trials and challenges in my life, I came to realize that God wants to be first because He loves us and wants to keep us alive and safe. He wants a relationship with His children.

If you are a parent, you can relate to that notion. Any good parent wants the best for their children. God is no different from us. He is the One who planted the seeds of who we are and how we react to our children with love. Even when our children go astray, we never stop caring for them and loving them.

In my youth, I was miserable because I did not have a close relationship with my dad, and I only cared about what God thought when times got tough. I played this silly game with God. When things were going well, I would put Him aside and think, "I'll call You if I need You, God." Sadly, I played this game with my dad as well. I had become complacent and prideful. I was immature and thought I could do everything on my own. I truly thought, "I don't need God or anyone giving me all their rules."

Oh, I am sure you can imagine what happened next. Yep! I hit a very low point in my life. You see, sometimes being at the bottom is the best place to be because the only place we have to go is up. I tell you it's not fun at the bottom. It hurts, and it can be very lonely. The feelings of desperation and hopelessness are overwhelming.

If you have ever experienced this, I am sure you can relate, and you know exactly what I am talking about. If you don't, just wait. Life without God is rough, and the world can be very cruel.

To make a long story short, I finally got my heart right with God, and He restored my relationship with my dad, family, and Himself. Looking back, when I tell my story to others, I feel like I am talking about someone else, and I start to feel sorry for the person I am speaking about. I must remind myself and the listener that I am no longer that person. The Lord has healed so many broken places in my life.

I want to focus back on the story of the Prodigal Son in the book of Luke. To start, the word *prodigal* means wasteful and reckless. In this story, the Prodigal Son took his inheritance and left the comforts of his home. He went looking for something he thought was better than what his father could provide. I can imagine him thinking, "That old man doesn't understand me; he's just old and has too many rules. I am ready to face the world and make something of myself apart from him. I will take all I have and go. I'll show him!"

It makes me laugh because how often do we hear youths say these very things? As adults, we know through our own life's experience that they have no clue what they're talking about. Yet we let them take their own path, hoping they will one day come to their senses and return home to our loving arms. Let's read the story from Luke 15:11–20 together:

The Parable of the Lost Son
Jesus continued: "There was a man who had two sons. The younger one said to his father, 'Father, give me my share of the estate.' So, he divided his property between them. Not long after that, the younger son got together all he had, set off for a distant country and there squandered his wealth in wild living. After he had spent everything, there was a severe famine in that whole country, and he began to be in

need. So, he went and hired himself out to a citizen of that country, who sent him to his fields to feed pigs. He longed to fill his stomach with the pods that the pigs were eating, but no one gave him anything. When he came to his senses, he said, 'How many of my father's hired servants have food to spare, and here I am starving to death! I will set out and go back to my father and say to him: Father, I have sinned against heaven and against you. I am no longer worthy to be called your son; make me like one of your hired servants.' So, he got up and went to his father. But while he was still a long way off, his father saw him and was filled with compassion for him; he ran to his son, threw his arms around him and kissed him." (Luke 15:11–20)

When I read the story of this lost son, I always get tears in my eyes. I can imagine the father waiting on the hill for his son. He wasn't off somewhere else; he was waiting in expectancy for his son to come down that long and winding road of life.

When reading this, I reflect on my own story. The day I "came to my senses," I set out to have a heart-to-heart conversation with my own dad. That day changed everything. It was one of the scariest and yet one of the best days of my life. I will never forget the words out of my dad's mouth. He said, "Ashley, I have been waiting for this day to come for years."

Those words shocked the heck out of me. I thought, "Really? Why have I been so afraid to have this conversation then?"

Before going into that conversation, I recall thinking that I was going to talk to my dad, give him an ultimatum, and leave there with nothing. But to my surprise, the opposite happened. He wrapped his arms around my neck and hugged me as we both had tears in our eyes. It was in that exact moment that I saw the reflection of God in my dad. This God that my dad loved so much was now my God, too.

Restoration and forgiveness took place that day, and we have never been the same since. I love talking to my dad and listening to all his wisdom. I trust him and take everything he says very seriously. I don't know what I would ever do without him.

It was also that day with my own dad that I understood how God is waiting for His children to come home to Him. I think back about that time when I was so desperate for God and how He never left me alone. Even when I thought I was running and hiding from Him, He knew everything and saw me with compassion. He heard every single one of my prayers and cries.

Like a good parent, Papa God isn't just ignoring us when we throw temper tantrums; He's waiting for us to calm down and come to our senses. He's patiently waiting for our hearts to change toward Him. That is spiritual maturity.

I truly believe that we live a lifetime to appreciate the people and relationships God has given us. More importantly, I am so grateful for the love and mercy of Papa God.

Here's the best part, and it's my favorite part of the story of the Prodigal Son. I truly hope it hits home with your heart, too.

> The son said to him, "Father, I have sinned against heaven and against you. I am no longer worthy to be called your son." But the father said to his servants, "Quick! Bring the best robe and put it on him. Put a ring on his finger and sandals on his feet. Bring the fattened calf and kill it. Let's have a feast and celebrate. For this son of mine was dead and is alive again; he was lost and is found." So, they began to celebrate. (Luke 15:21–24)

Friend, do you notice the father's reaction when his son came home? The father told everyone that his son was back, and they had a great celebration.

Only the best would do for this lost son who was now found. He treated him with so much love, and he was excited to see his son. He knew his son had done some detestable things while gone, but he didn't care. He was just happy that he had come to his senses and was now back at home. That is exactly how Papa God feels about His children when we repent of our sins and come to God through Jesus. He treats us as though we never sinned and we are royalty in His eyes.

I can't even begin to explain how awesome my life is. The very thing I was running from is the very thing I can't live without. I am so glad that we serve a God who is full of grace and love for us. He is a forgiving God and a God of restoration.

If my story has touched your heart and you feel it is like yours, stop and spend time with Papa God. He wants to speak to you about this story and reveal His plans for your life. If it will help you, go read the story again about the lost son in Luke 15:1–31.

When you read it, reflect on your own life and think about how many times the Father (who really is Papa God in this parable) has been waiting on the hill for you. He loves you so much, and He is a patient God. He is a God of restoration. Remember, if you have hit rock bottom, there is no better time than right now to look up. He is waiting with open arms for you to come home. No matter what you have done, it is no surprise to God. He knows everything, and He is faithful to forgive. "If we confess our sins, he is faithful and just and will forgive us our sins and purify us from all unrighteousness" (1 John 1:9).

This story was very difficult for me to write. I cried the whole time, not with sadness, but with thanksgiving to Papa God and for the prayers of my parents. If you are a parent with a prodigal, don't give up. Keep praying for your child to come home to the Lord. Prayer works!

For the prodigal reading this: My prayer for you is that one day you will be able to reflect on your old life and know how much God truly loves you. You're not lost. You have always been found. Just look up!

Big hugs,
Papa God and Ashley

Ladybug Dream and Wasabi!

In 2012, Branch of Christ Church had a women's retreat out in the country. Before I arrived at the retreat, I was singing in my car while listening to a song by Natalie Grant called, "Beauty Mark."

I thought about an ugly beauty mark I had removed from the back of my leg when I was in my mid-twenties. It would get caught when I went down the slides in the park when I was a little girl. Then, while I was pregnant with my oldest daughter, a blood clot formed under the beauty mark that looked horrible. I told God, "I am glad I had that nasty-looking thing removed." Thinking figuratively about the song by Natalie Grant, I continued, "I guess I will now wear that beauty mark on my face for You, God."

Then I heard the Lord say in my spirit, "Ashley, you need to laugh."

His response kind of stumped me for a moment. I thought, *That was an interesting statement.* Yet, I went along and drove to the retreat with a sense of zeal in anticipation of what God had planned for the other ladies and me.

During the first church service, the move of God was so great that the ladies in attendance were set free from past sins and afflictions with which the enemy had tried to keep them bound. I know this because after the retreat, we all spoke openly about what God had done for us. The atmosphere was thick with the presence of the Holy Spirit.

One of the guest speakers, a strong woman of God named Bonita, touched my heart. She gave me a picture of a precious little girl that she had kept in her Bible. The little girl was bent over and smiling as she looked at a beautiful butterfly. She was dressed in blue jean overalls, a pale pink shirt, with cute little pink ribbons in her soft pigtails, and she was standing on green grass in her bare feet. There was so much detail in this picture that would soon be a revelation for me from God.

Unaware of what I heard that morning from God and the song I sang about the beauty mark, Bonita had used a black ink pen to put a mole on the face of this little girl. Curious, I asked her why she put that dot on the picture and she said, "A good friend of mine gave me this picture a few months ago. She knew that I liked overalls and how sweet the little girl looked, so she thought of me." She said, "I believe God wanted me to know that He saw me, and I put that little black mole on the face of the little girl myself because it represented purity as I was claiming the rights of the little girl's innocence without fear."

Even though the mole or birthmark meant something completely different to each of us, it was still mind-blowing that God used it to connect Bonita and me. After that retreat, the Lord revealed more to me about that picture regarding the transformation in me that weekend. He showed me that I, too, am seen by God, and He wanted me to know I am His little girl. The picture was a visual example of me looking at the transformation He was working in me. Who could have known at the time that one day I would include this experience in a book He asked me to write called, *Papa God and Ashley*? Isn't God awesome? But just wait, this testimony is even better than that! God was about to put together more of this puzzle for me through Bonita and another strong woman of God named Victoria.

That night, we stayed in quiet little cabins. I prayed and asked God to reveal what His plans were for me. He had told me a few years earlier that I would work with abused and abandoned children one day. However, at that time, I did not know where God was leading me or how to accomplish it. I just knew in my heart that if God had it planned and promised it, I was certain it had to be something more magnificent than I could imagine or think at the time. It wasn't until April 2015 (three years later) that God would open the door for me to become an advocate and a signed artist for Holt International Children's Services. And that is entirely another story only possibly by divine intervention.

During an altar call the next day, I asked Victoria to pray for me because I needed to know how to move forward in what God wanted me to do with my life.

Suddenly, Victoria held up her hand in front of my face (she did not touch me) and yelled, *"That's the prophetic!"*

I felt like something smacked me upside the forehead. Without a thought, I fell to the ground, prostrate. The power of the Holy Spirit reminded me of a scene in a movie when a bomb goes off and the blast flings a person down. I know that sounds a little dramatic, but that is how it felt to me. The Holy Spirit hit me so hard that as I lay there, I started laughing hysterically for what seemed like two or three hours. I was crying and laughing at the same time, and I was glued to the floor and unable to stand back up. Believe me, I tried but was unsuccessful. The interesting part is I was shouting out, *"Wasabi!"* I was thinking, "Man, this is a powerful feeling!" referring to the feeling that had come on me by the Holy Spirit. Remember when God told me I need to laugh? I had no idea that this was what He was thinking of. When I heard this in my spirit that morning prior, I thought, "Oh, a nice giggle with some of the other ladies." *But no!* I was laughing like I had never laughed before, and I was praying in the natural realm and in the spirit.

OK. Let's pause in this story because I can hear it now. Some of you may be thinking, "Whatever, Ashley. This is sounding really out there." But I am asking you to keep reading; I know that my testimony is going to open your eyes. Keep in mind that God abides in the supernatural realm, not in the natural realm like we do. The Lord specifically told me in prayer to write this. If you have started reading this already, that means it is most likely for you.

It is very important to mention that we can say we love God and appreciate His Son, but there are people who want to dismiss the move of the Holy Spirit. If we do this, we are rejecting the Holy Trinity. This is like saying, "I like the way you look and you seem nice, but I don't want anything to do with your personality." That's rude and rooted in fear, which stops the move of what God wants to do in our lives, leaving us stalled or frozen when the Holy Spirit wants us to move as He moves in us and through us. And every time He moves in us, He always points us back to Jesus.

One of the jobs of the Holy Spirit is to bring understanding so He can help us, and we can help others. When we allow the Holy Spirit to move in us, healing and transformation can take place in our lives. "Do not quench the Spirit. Do not treat prophecies with contempt but test them all; hold on to what is good, reject every kind of evil" (1 Thess. 5:19–22).

There are those who witnessed me falling to the ground as many others were laughing with me because it was hysterical watching my great belly laugh. There is something about laughter that is contagious and healing. I could not control what was happening, and I so desperately wanted to share this feeling with others around me. Pastor Debra Kaplan even came up to me at one point and said, "More, God! Give her *more!*"

Every time she did this, I would feel a rush of what I called wasabi (power) fill my entire body to the point of feeling that I might explode somehow. I kept saying, "Oh no, don't do that! That is way too much for my physical body to handle!"

To give you a full understanding of that night, I must tell you that on the other side of the room was a lady who was experiencing the same thing. But she wasn't laughing; she was fervently crying out to God. It was like we were undergoing a polar opposite experience. When I spoke to her the next day, she told me the Lord was healing her emotionally, and all she could do was cry. The Lord was healing something inside of me, too, but for some reason, I laughed. I also think He was giving me joy to laugh at the enemy because Satan is already defeated by the blood of Jesus.

When the night was over and the group of ladies was ready to go to bed, I was still lying on the ground but finally starting to feel like I could stand up again. My body felt heavy, so I had to ask some of the other women to help me get up off the ground. They were telling me, "We've got to go to bed, Ashley. It's late."

As I walked back to my cabin, I started to feel embarrassed, realizing what had just happened. Thoughts came in my head like, "Oh my gosh! You looked so stupid laughing hysterically on the ground and shouting 'wasabi!' What is wrong with you? You must think this is the Ashley Show or something. These ladies are going to think you are crazy."

Fear and doubt started to engulf all my emotions. The attack of thoughts became more and more intense. One thought I recall that really got to me was, "Why can't you be soft-spoken like so and so? She is so sweet and nice, and you are loud and obnoxious, Ashley. Everyone was staring at you as you were making a total fool of yourself."

Tears filled my eyes thinking about these lies from the enemy. I prayed and asked God to help me. I started having a full-blown pity party for myself. As we were getting settled in our rooms, people were still talking about what happened to me. After everything settled down the next day, I realized that they weren't talking about me negatively.

They were talking and laughing about how it was so amazing to see what God was doing in me and through me. They, too, had their own encounters with the Holy Spirit, and some admitted later that seeing what happened to me made them want to experience God on this level.

Going back to the pity party I was having: Everyone settled into their beds, and I could hear others talking and enjoying each other's company. Not me! I lay in my bed feeling defeated and ridiculous. Negative thoughts were beating on me as I drifted off to sleep.

Then, in the middle of the night, I had a dream. The dream started out like an old-fashioned movie, you know, the ones with the number countdown in a circular motion? It was like a Doppler radar going around in a circle with numbers after each full circle was completed.

The picture I could see started a countdown of five, four, three, two, and one. Then I could hear the ticking of the film, and the movie began. I saw a ladybug in a big open field with bright green grass. It was a beautiful day with a nice breeze, and the sun was shining. There were a few trees over to the right of the field.

This cute little ladybug fluttered from blade of grass to blade of grass. I could tell it was just enjoying the sunshine and breeze. She was fluttering along very happily. Then, suddenly, I could see something in the distance that camouflaged itself to look like a blade of grass. It was an ugly praying mantis waiting for the little ladybug to flutter over to him and land on him. In my dream, I could tell it was up to something bad.

Still in the dream, I started yelling, "No little ladybug, don't go over there! It's not a blade of grass. It is an insect trying to deceive you to eat you!"

As I cried out this warning to the ladybug, I saw two masculine but gentle hands come out of the cloudy sky. Just before the ladybug reached the grass impostor, the hands scooped it up and I heard, "You see, Ashley, I've got you. Just like this little ladybug, I made you unique for a purpose. I've got you in the palms of my hands, and I have great plans for you."

Then the Lord told me to get up and open my Bible to read 1 Corinthians 12. I woke up and my Bible was sitting on the sink counter near the bathroom. Now, the funny thing is, I didn't even know where this was in the Bible because I was still half asleep. But I immediately turned the pages and landed right on 1 Corinthians 12. That surprised me, too. The Lord specifically had me read verses 7–14.

Now to each one the manifestation of the Spirit is given for the common good. To one there is given through the Spirit a message of wisdom, to another a message of knowledge by means of the same Spirit, to another faith by the same Spirit, to another gift of healing by that one Spirit, to another miraculous power, to another prophecy, to another distinguishing between spirits, to another speaking in different kinds of tongues, and to still another the interpretation of tongues. All these are the work of one and the same Spirit, and he distributes them to each one, just as he determines. Just as a body, though one, has many parts, but all its many parts form one body, so it is with Christ. For we were all baptized by one Spirit so as to form one body—whether Jews or Gentiles, slave or free—and we were all given the one Spirit to drink. Even so the body is not made up of one part but of many. (1 Cor. 12:7–14)

The next morning, I woke up so excited about my dream and what the Lord had shared with me. I went to Pastor Debra Kaplan and asked if I could get up and speak to the women at the retreat. The Lord told me to explain this Scripture on spiritual gifts to the ladies. I somehow knew that some of the ladies had no idea what had happened to me and the other lady who was lying on the ground crying the night before.

The Lord wanted us to know that we are all made for a purpose, and He has known us throughout our whole lives, even when we were little children. He used me and the other lady to demonstrate not only His power, but His love for each of us. The message was clear: Even if we don't look and act like someone else, God gave us all different gifts for the purpose and fulfillment of the body of Christ. Satan will always try to disguise the situation to deceive us to take our eyes off the purpose for which God created us.

God does not want us to be anyone other than who He made us to be. If you're very talkative like I am, it's OK. He will use that gift if you are willing to trust Him and step out on a stage to speak of and for Him. If you're shy and soft spoken, it's OK. He has a big plan for even the softest-spoken person. God often speaks in a soft whisper like it says in 1 Kings 19:11–13.

Trust that God has a plan for you with whatever talents He has given you. If you don't know what your purpose is, ask God to show you. Oh, and don't worry. I don't think the Holy Spirit is going to make you shout wasabi and have you laughing hysterically for hours on the floor. The Holy Spirit is always a gentleman and will never go against our free will. He obviously needed to make a statement, and He knew I would be open and willing to be that person. The honor is worth it for me to be used by the Lord, even if I felt like a fool for a short time. Something deep happened to me that night with Papa God, and I haven't been the same person ever since. My self-confidence went up, and I know who I am to my Lord and King, Jesus.

I am so glad we are all made differently. If we were all the same, imagine what a boring world it would be! Trust that God made you unique for His glory and honor. It really doesn't matter what others think of us anyway. What matters is what God thinks about us and if we are living the life that He has called us to live.

He loves you so much, ladybug! Reflecting on the picture of the little girl looking at the butterfly, I can see how God is transforming each of us into whom He has called us to be on this earth. Can you see this transformation happening in you? Just wait, it only gets better from here. Papa God has great plans for you.

P.S. There are male ladybugs, too. They're not all girls. But of course, you already knew that!

Big hugs,
Papa God and Ashley

Tie Your Shoelaces

While I was traveling on a family vacation, I saw a kid who had his shoes untied. The Holy Spirit started to teach me something through this kid's untied shoes. In this illustration, the Old and New Testaments are the shoelaces in a spiritual sense. The shoelaces also represent the wisdom only God can provide through our time with Him reading the Bible. I love when Papa God gives me a visual for something pertaining to the spirit realm, and I want to share it with you. So I will start with a question for you to consider.

Spiritually, are your shoes tied, or are you walking around with your laces dangling and dragging the ground? Before you can answer this question, let me explain a few things. I will ask you this question again near the end of the chapter.

"Be careful, you might trip over your shoelaces," my mom would say to me when I was a young girl and just learning to tie my own shoes.

Shoelaces come together and tie both sides, binding the tie in a bow for the purpose of holding the content inside, meaning that the lace is all one piece but it is woven throughout the shoe in different segments. As I thought on this, the Lord led me to Scripture in the Old Testament, and I thought of a metaphor of how the Bible has important content from God for us when I was reading Daniel 7:14.

To set the stage, Daniel was disclosing a vision of what many Bible scholars believe is about the last days of this age, signifying a window of time. Daniel writes about this revelation and of all that would happen in the end. The Son of Man, Jesus, would have the final authority that would be given to Him and to the body of Christ through His birth, death, and resurrection. *This authority binds us to the Father's plan by restoring the broken tie of sin in preparation for finalizing the original plan from the beginning.* This plan for redemption is found in Genesis 3:15 through Revelation 20. This is the written plan of the final victory that triumphs over our enemy, the devil, and his world system. Daniel's vision is one of the signs in Scripture that Jesus would have the final authority that would never be destroyed.

Daniel writes about his vision:

> I kept looking in the night visions, and behold, with the clouds of heaven one like a Son of Man was coming, and He came up to the Ancient of Days and was presented before Him. And to Him was given dominion, glory and a kingdom, that all the peoples, nations, and men of every language might serve Him. His dominion is an everlasting dominion which will not pass away, and His kingdom is one which will not be destroyed. (Dan. 7:13–14 AMP)

This great promise was written between approximately 605 and 535 BC, around twenty-five centuries ago. This prophecy is just one of hundreds that tie the Old Testament and New Testaments together.

God created a new covenant through Jesus in the New Testament. Another way to say this is: the old agreement and the new agreement between God and mankind. Everything in the Old Testament is fulfilled in the New Testament, and the New Testament ties up the Old Testament like a big beautiful bow that is woven throughout the generations. The new agreement is the fulfillment of the promises of God through Jesus.

I have heard people say, "I only want to focus on the New Testament. The Old doesn't apply to me because of what Jesus did to save me from my sins." But if we are only looking at one or the other, we can't see the big picture God wants us to understand and to put into action.

You might be asking, "Why is this important, Ashley?" Well get ready, I am about to tell you.

If you don't correlate the Old Testament and the New Testament when you study Scripture, you will stumble and fall in your belief and faith. How could there be a need for anything new if we can't look back on the old way of things and appreciate what Jesus did? They are not meant to be without each other because the story would be incomplete. No matter how we look at it, it is impossible to tie one side of the shoelace by itself or even cut one side off and discard it.

The Bible is history written over a span of two thousand years; it has sixty-six books, written on three different continents and in three different languages by forty different authors. Think about that for a second. Many of these authors never read what the other authors had written. Their similar stories are astounding and could only be possible by the hand of divine intervention. The facts sketched throughout history alone are worth the research to understand who this God of the universe is and why He so desperately made sure His children had a way back to Him after Adam and Eve committed high treason—the sin resulting in the great divide between God and man. God went to great lengths to have His beloved back legally and in a right standing with Him.

God's desire is that you understand why it is important to read all sixty-six books in the Bible as one complete story. Don't feel overwhelmed by this statement. You can read it in bite-size sections and at your own pace. The point is for you to read it and allow the Holy Spirit to guide you where He wants you to gain His wisdom and understanding.

Here is another comparison to shoelaces about the wisdom gained from the Old and New Testaments. Imagine starting from a slow walk, accelerating into a fast-paced stride, and then to go faster, you speed up to a full-blown sprint. Left untied, your shoe will eventually fall off, leaving you shoeless and hobbling, exposing you to the harsh elements of the world.

Every time we slip and fall we must tie those laces and keep running the race set before us at a pace that is comfortable, yet steady. The way to tie those laces spiritually is through time devoted to studying the Word of God and putting the Word into action in our lives.

We can't just do a little here and a little there and leave the rest unlaced. Reading only parts of Scripture would be incomplete and pointless. There is no true wisdom in doing this; it's essentially being negligent. You would have a fact based on an assumption of partial, unresearched information in an effort to know the whole truth. Like my friend Carman says, "You can't pick apart one continuous shoelace; it's all one piece."

Let me explain more about incomplete wisdom. Have you ever spoken to someone who misunderstands or guesses a Scripture, and by the way they are talking, you know they have no clue what they're talking about? They have parts of it right, and then they make up other parts just trying to make sense of what they believe they're saying. You know that they have never really studied the topic in the Word. You conclude that they are just going based on hearsay. That is very frustrating to the person who knows the truth and has read the Scriptures themselves.

Oh, I am not bashing those people who misunderstand; I have been that person, and I have also been the person who knows the truth because I read what the Bible said on a matter. The frustrating part is when they are determined that they know the answer based on a hypothesis without listening to reason.

I have been caught coming up with my own interpretation. Feeling clueless during the conversation, I wasn't happy with myself, and that is what drove me to go read Scripture on that particular subject on my own time. Once the truth was understood, I then had to go back and rectify my error or I repented to God when the option to go back to that person wasn't available. Finding out the truth makes sure you are not misguided or misguiding others with an assumption. Changing what God said can be very dangerous. (See Rev. 22:18–19.)

That's why it is so important to read the whole Bible yourself— Genesis to Revelation—and not just take someone's word for it. Take your Bible to church with you even if the church puts the Scriptures on the big screen or in a study guide. If your pastor knows the Word of God well, he or she will jump back and forth between the Old and New Testaments, tying them together. With today's technology, we can pull up Scripture on our phones with a Bible app. During the service, read the Scripture along with your pastor and take notes to research on your own. You want to make sure that what is being taught is God's truth, not human interpretation. There is a lot of false information out there, and if someone is not teaching that Jesus is the only way, they are false prophets spreading false teachings. Please read the following Scriptures to better understand false prophets: Matthew 24:11, 24; 1 John 4:1; and 2 Peter 2:1–3.

If you are learning about a subject that is foreign to you, ask the Holy Spirit to give you understanding and wisdom on that subject. Go directly to the source of wisdom. The Holy Spirit is the One who wrote the Bible anyway. (See 2 Tim. 3:16, 2 Peter 1:20–21.)

This discussion reminds me of the telephone game. Someone says something in a sermon or conversation, and they add to what the Word says. The person who doesn't know what God said takes the discussion as truth without researching it on their own. Then they go tell another person and so on and so on it goes. A new way of thinking is birthed and deception is created.

You know the saying, "I swear to tell the truth the whole truth and nothing but the truth, so help me God." Without the whole truth, it is nothing but a twisted-up lie with some truth mixed in. I like the example of the shoelaces, but in this case, the laces of lies or misunderstandings are jumbled up into a gigantic messed up knot!

Soon, someone who is a deceiver or one who is deceived and doesn't know the Word, comes along and will say, "Did God really say that?" or "That just can't be true, I've never heard that verse like that before, and it sure doesn't apply to me." This lack of knowledge and thinking is dangerous for their eternal existence. It is written in Scripture that there is no excuse for not knowing the truth. "My people are destroyed from lack of knowledge. "Because you have rejected knowledge, I also reject you as my priests; because you have ignored the law of your God, I also will ignore your children" (Hos. 4:6).

If you don't understand the full truth, chances are you will be deceived just like Eve was in the Garden of Eden when the snake asked her if she could eat from the tree of knowledge of good and evil.

> Now the serpent was more crafty than any of the wild animals the Lord God had made. He said to the woman, "Did God really say, 'You must not eat from any tree in the garden?'" The woman said to the serpent, "We may eat fruit from the trees in the garden, but God did say, 'You must not eat fruit from the tree that is in the middle of the garden, and you must not touch it, or you will die.'" "You will not certainly die," the serpent said to the woman. (Gen. 3:1–4)

Now would you just look at that! Eve added something to the law about the Tree of the Knowledge of Good and Evil. She added, "We can't even *touch* the tree!" God didn't say they couldn't touch it. I am sure

Adam may have said something like, "Just avoid it, Eve, and don't even go over there." But like every misinterpretation since, somebody adds to God's Word or takes what they want out of it and leaves the rest for someone else to figure out. I think this is because they either like their sin and don't want to change, or they want to be self-deceived so they can say they didn't know and acknowledge their wrong thinking. Either way, Satan is a liar and he led Eve to believe a twisted truth within a lie.

So let's look at what God did say to Adam back in Genesis 2:16–17. "And the Lord God commanded the man, 'You are free to eat from any tree in the garden; but you must not eat from the tree of the knowledge of good and evil, for when you eat from it you will certainly die'" (Gen. 2:16–17).

See how Satan got Eve and Adam all mixed up? The lie from Satan was that he twisted what God said about good and evil that she wouldn't certainly die, meaning physically—well, at least not right way.

I know this sounds terrible to say, but I can envision Adam standing nearby cringing as he looked to see if Eve keeled over after she bit the fruit. Since she didn't, he ate it, too. Oh yes, Adam was standing there. Eve wasn't alone with the snake because Scripture says that she gave some to her husband. (See Gen. 3:6.) There is no finger-pointing allowed here. They both ate the fruit of sin. The rotten part was Adam knew it was wrong because God told him directly, whereas Eve was deceived by her interpretation of what she was told.

What Adam should have remembered from his conversations with God was that sin is separation from eternal life with God. Not only did they die spiritually, they eventually died physically, but it had nothing to do with touching the fruit. It had to do with their disobedience and ingesting the sin. Satan convinced them that if they wanted to know what God knows, all they had to do is take a bite, and their eyes would be opened. "'You will not certainly die,'" the serpent said to the woman. 'For God knows that when you eat from it your eyes will be opened, and you will be like God, knowing good and evil'" (Gen. 3:4–5). Well, they found out, didn't they? Sin will kill, and so their bodies went into deterioration mode; its ripple effect impacts all humanity until we meet Jesus. (See 2 Cor. 5:1–10.)

We need to understand that Satan said a partial truth, but he twisted it in a way that seemed desirable to them. Because of their desire to know sin, the deterioration of their bodies just took longer than what they thought, and it wasn't an immediate or drastic reaction. Isn't that what happens with sin still today?

We hear wise people say to the unwise, "Don't smoke or drink that; it will kill you." Maybe that person doesn't physically or spiritually die right away but eventually, it will catch up to them. They want instant gratification and try it anyway. Then they are hooked into a sin that is detrimental to their bodies and their fellowship with God. Then this don't-do-it sin is what separates them from the Word of God that is meant to save them and set them free from a life full of pain and disappointment. The enemy has them bound in their sin, and they feel unworthy to be in the presence of a holy God. Thank God, we walk by faith and not how we feel.

The reason I used this story of Eve eating the fruit is to illustrate that the tactics of the enemy never change. Satan still uses the same forms of manipulation to con people into questioning what God said. The good news is that God gave us a manual with all the help we need to understand what happened and what will happen from the beginning to the end, Genesis to Revelation. All the answers are there at your fingertips. The enemy wants nothing more than to trip you up, confuse you, or stop you from reading. Without fail, he will send all kinds of interruptions in your time with God. Don't allow distractions during your time with Him. This is your time to learn from and to be loved by Him.

If you do trip over your shoelaces and tumble, don't worry, get back up, and brush yourself off. Get your Bible out and ask God for forgiveness and repent of the mistake. Kneel to pray and lace back up the correct way. Your Papa God will be there to kiss your scraped knees. He will give you wisdom through the Holy Spirit, and He will teach you to tie the laces just right.

The Bible is the ultimate love story between our Creator and His beloved children. He loves us so much that He wants to show us how He tied this life story together to keep us safe and always ready for the next step. The Holy Spirit is ready and willing to guide your every move. He will never leave you to stay untied or tangled in deception, but you have a part to play in this story of redemption. No one can do it for you.

Check those spiritual shoelaces (wisdom gained from the Old and New Testaments) and make sure they are tied in preparation to skip, jump, and even run through this life with joy and gladness that the Lord has planned for you. He knows the whole story from beginning to end. He is not holding back any secrets from us. He wants us to know what happened and what is to come. "I have told you these things so that in me you may have peace. In this world, you will have trouble. But take heart! I have overcome the world" (John 16:33).

I can imagine seeing what Daniel saw—Jesus coming back in those clouds of heaven with the finish line just ahead. With the story told ahead of time, we should get excited. For the end of this great love story already tells us that we win against the deception of Satan and his world kingdom. It is written. We win in the end! "Look, he is coming with the clouds," and "every eye will see him, even those who pierced him"; and all peoples on earth "will mourn because of him." So shall it be! Amen" (Rev. 1:7).

I pray that these illustrations help you to see the bigger picture and the plans of God to be fulfilled in the earth from the fall of Adam to the first coming of Jesus and His return.

One last morsel I would like to recommend is that you can buy the Bible on CDs and listen to Scripture. It's another perspective that helps the stories come to life. The one I own is *Bible Alive* in the *New Living Translation*. I like to listen to them while I am sitting somewhere waiting to fill time. But don't just listen to the Word, be a doer of it. Apply the Word of God to your everyday life. If you do, it will mold your life into all God has called you to become.

Most of the time before I stand up and speak at an event, I will write a note or say a prayer. I say, "Papa, let's change the world!" It is a great reminder of whom I represent and why I am there in the first place. It is only through the time I spend with the Lord reading, praying, and worshiping, that it is possible for me to be His representative to those who need to know Jesus. There is a lot of work to be done before His return, and I am honored to be used by the Lord for His glory.

OK, now! Are you ready to answer my question? Are your shoelaces tied, or are they dangling and dragging the ground? It's up to you and the Holy Spirit to work on tying them up. Throughout this book, I will give you Scriptures along the way to seek out the truth for yourself. Don't avoid reading them, or you will miss important pieces of the story. The purpose of this book is to help establish your relationship with God through Jesus and the wisdom of the Holy Spirit. Again, it's not my relationship that will matter when you stand before God one day. (See 2 Cor. 5:10.) You will be held responsible for your relationship, and I will be held responsible for my relationship with Him. But I am glad you are coming along with me in these writings to seek what Papa God wants to teach you. Come along with me and find out the way to your final destination.

Big hugs,
Papa God and Ashley

GPS to Final Destination Lane

Did you know that a GPS (global positioning system) can't tell you where to go until you start moving? Have you ever noticed that? We plug in the destination into the GPS, and once the vehicle or person moves, the directions pop up on the screen. At that moment, a signal is sent to the satellite in outer space. Then and only then do we have directions to where we are going. A voice comes on the GPS and starts the route. Sometimes the GPS will announce that the directions may be missing some steps along the way, or it will mention that there may be gated access that could limit the traveler's entry.

Here's a secret that many Christians don't know or fully understand. God can't move unless we move first. Prayer is like a GPS; I call it our global prayer system. This kind of GPS has better directions than any man-made monitoring device. It has also been around far longer.

This kind of GPS comes from within our thoughts and spirit man who connects to the Holy Spirit by sending out prayers that ascend into the throne room of heaven to Jesus Himself. The Holy Spirit is our helper and His directions are like the satellite. I like to think of the Holy

Spirit as the power and voice on the GPS helping us along the way like it says in 1 Corinthians 2:4–5.

In John 16, before Jesus sat down at the right hand of the Father, He had a conversation with His disciples and gave them verbal instructions essentially saying, "Don't travel until I send you a traveling companion who will help lead you in the right direction. This companion works and walks alongside you as a GPS and has great power and wisdom. You will need Him to go with you along your journey. There is a mission I have planned for you to take, but wait before you go, I will send you this helper first. The path is long with many detours. There are enemies who will try their hardest to send you off course from the correct path and even try to wreck the mission. But if you listen to Him and pay close attention, the Holy Spirit will show you the way to truth. If you don't take Him with you, you risk getting lost along the way, and you will just keep going in a vicious circle."

The Work of the Holy Spirit
When the Advocate comes, whom I will send to you from the Father—the Spirit of truth who goes out from the Father—he will testify about me. And you also must testify, for you have been with me from the beginning. (John 15:26–27)

Exalted to the right hand of God, he has received from the Father the promised Holy Spirit and has poured out what you now see and hear. (Acts 2:33)

Friend, we pray for many different reasons, but one reason is that we are asking God where to go or what to do next. For those of us who are visual, a good example is how to get from point A to point B, like a parade in a big city. There is a beginning and ending with a story line in between. But the destination is always for the will and purpose of God that He may be glorified through every situation.

We pray because we know God has superior wisdom and understanding, but we are lacking in our own foggy wisdom and understanding. What we need is His revelation truth as described in 1 Corinthians 2:9–10 and 2:16.

My friend Katherine Jones says that, "God has a bird's-eye view of everything happening around us, and He can see the beginning to the end in every situation." She explained it to me like this: "Imagine a parade going along in a big city. God can see far above the parade. He knows the start of the parade and where it should end. There are turns to take and turns to be avoided that would cause us to get off the appointed course. We must trust God and listen to His wisdom to make it safely to the end of the parade."

One day I was having a conversation with my friend Tashia. I explained Kathy's analogy to her and she said, "I feel like that bird's-eye view analogy is the dove that represents the Holy Spirit, the Spirit of Truth." She got it! See how God works! I love fresh revelation, and Papa God will even lead us to people along the way to show us that we are on the right or wrong course.

Here's my point: When we pray, we are asking for God's viewpoint because He can see far above our circumstances. We pray for wisdom because we need to know what we should do in those situations to guide us to the final destination. That is why it's imperative that we have godly friends we can trust and know they have our backs. "This is what the LORD says, he who made the earth, the LORD who formed it and established it—the LORD is his name: 'Call to me and I will answer you and tell you great and unsearchable things you do not know'" (Jer. 33:2–3).

Often on the journey of life, we want to take a shorter route without knowing exactly where it leads. Maybe this method has worked for us, but many times we get lost along the way and then we must call someone or pull over and ask for directions. Much time has been wasted, and frustration sets in for the traveler.

There have been times in my life that Papa God was asking me to take a new path that seemed longer than I anticipated and too intense for me to travel on my own. It seemed as though I would never find the end of the journey. Hypothetically, the path had mountains, valleys, twists, and turns. The spiritual weather seemed like a storm was coming, and I longed to get to the other side where the sun was shining.

Faith and trust represent our left and right in the directions. If we go by our own understanding, the directions can get turned around and we turn down Confusion Circle on our path to Final Destination Lane. Roadblocks and missing steps turn us around and keep us off the path that would get us there quickly and safely. When we see this happening, we must stop and think, "Is this the path the Lord wants me to take, or am I trying to redirect His path for my purpose and personal glory?" When we try to take over the wheel of control we are called a backseat driver. We need to check ourselves and make sure our motives are right when we are praying to God for the answers.

> You desire but do not have, so you kill. You covet but you cannot get what you want, so you quarrel and fight. You do not have because you do not ask God. (James 4:2)

> Trust in the Lord with all your heart and lean not on your own understanding; in all your ways submit to him, and he will make your paths straight. (Prov. 3:5–6)

It's time to let Jesus take over in the driver's seat and turn on your global praying system so that the Spirit of truth can lead the way. The Lord has great plans for each of us. Trust that He knows the way. Trust Him, but remember it's up to you and me to start moving. Ask Papa

God, "What is our next address toward the destination, and how do we get there?" He's ready to go when you are.

With that said, it is important to know how to hear the voice of God when He is speaking to you, correct? Well then, we are off to the next chapter!

Big hugs,
Papa God and Ashley

The Voice of God

Do you hear the voice of God speaking to you? Or are you running so fast that you can't hear Him? I am just as guilty as the next person when it comes to this.

I have cried out for answers in prayer but haven't taken the time to stop and listen to what God has to say about it.

At times, I think part of it is because I wasn't conditioned to hear His voice. There are many other reasons as well. Some may think they're on their own, and His answers are not going to be good enough. When we are doing something wrong, maybe we don't really want to hear His answer because it doesn't fit our desires and schedule. We become desensitized to His voice by ignoring Him.

I assume that most people really aren't trying to ignore God. They are conditioned, because of habit, to ask others for advice, thinking they have the answers. They need that one-on-one communication, and they fully trust the other person's wisdom.

Whatever the reason is, we are a busy generation. I call this generation the microwave age. It's the, "I need what I need, now" generation." We are running as fast as we can, here and there in a hurry, and for what?

You might say, "I don't know, but I've got to get there. When I arrive, I'll figure it out, and then I will just know." Any of these scenarios can be a dangerous way to think, and if not handled in a way that glorifies God, could be disastrous to our lives and others in our lives.

Have you ever just wanted to get somewhere fast and then realized you must wait because it wasn't what you expected or it was just the wrong time? The person who gave you the information you were seeking turned out to be incorrect, and now you're at a standstill or dead end. We put pressure on ourselves and others to hurry and wait. That is not only frustrating, but the pressure makes other people change their schedules to accommodate the situation that was not necessary in the first place.

In 1 Kings 19, Elijah was running for his life from Queen Jezebel. He was afraid she was going to kill him because he had just conquered her army and made a spectacle of her prophets. God had brought fire down from heaven and consumed a sacrifice of a bull in front of all the people, showing His power and majesty to everyone. In 1 Kings 18:38 we see that the fire consumed the sacrifice, the wood, the stones, and the soil, and it licked the water from the trench. God literally left nothing behind. I don't know about you, but I think this would have been really amazing and impressive to witness. Elijah had the almighty God on his side, and he was still afraid and ready to run from this evil woman. Later, in 1 Kings 19:9, Elijah hid from her in a cave, afraid that she would find him and kill him.

It sounds ridiculous, but don't make fun of him. We have all been there a time or two ourselves. Someone has hurt our feelings, or even worse, like Elijah, someone may have threatened to take our lives or livelihood. In the natural realm, I would be putting on my running shoes and taking off into the desert to hide, too.

Elijah was looking at the situation in the natural realm, not by faith, knowing that no matter what was happening in his life, God was about to do another miracle. I am not sure what Elijah was thinking when he was running away (off his path), except that maybe it would get better when he hid in the desert; he was just hoping to get away from the situation. God had to call him out and ask him why he was hiding.

Have we ever stopped to think, "What am I running from that God can't handle?" When I read about this experience, I can imagine Elijah crying out to God for help. After all, he had just witnessed God bring fire down from heaven, so he knew firsthand the power of God.

Finally, when Elijah found shelter in a cave, he cried out to God, and God answered him. But to Elijah's surprise, God's didn't speak in a booming voice.

> After the earthquake came a fire, but the Lord was not in the fire. And after the fire came a gentle whisper. When Elijah heard it, he pulled his cloak over his face and went out and stood at the mouth of the cave. Then a voice said to him, "What are you doing here, Elijah?" He replied, "I have been very zealous for the Lord God Almighty. The Israelites have rejected your covenant, torn down your altars, and put your prophets to death with the sword. I am the only one left, and now they are trying to kill me too." (1 Kings 19:12–14)

I'm not saying Elijah didn't have a good reason of his own to run and hide; his life was in real danger. Jezebel thought she had killed all the other prophets of God, and Elijah was the last one left. He was scared. (See 1 Kings 18:4.)

What I'm saying is where are we going in such a hurry that we can't stop for a minute to ask God what to do and say what's going on in our lives? The enemy wants us to be afraid; if we are disconnected from the voice of God, then he has us right where he wants us, alone in the desert.

I would like to tell on myself. One day I was driving in my car with a friend of mine, Joni. We were pulling out of a parking lot to visit a client. Because the streets were built in half-mile blocks, I had a choice to take a left or right to get to my destination and either way could get me there. In my mind, it was safer to turn right instead of going across three lanes of traffic to turn left and go the back way.

I heard a still, small voice in my spirit that said, "Go left, it's safer." But I was in a hurry, and I chose to ignore that voice since my own rationality told me that turning right was a faster and safer route. I took a right and went about two hundred yards after I had merged into the far-left lane. A lady was pulling out of an apartment community trying to go across all the lanes and turn left.

Before I go on with the rest of the story, can I tell you how much I loved my car? It was my first really nice car, and I even named her Lola because she was so pretty. I worked hard to buy that car, and I always took exceptionally good care of it. I had a funny saying: "What Lola wants, Lola gets!"

Anyway, I saw this lady pull out of her community and come toward me, but there was nowhere for me to go to avoid her. I knew she was about to run right into me. Her car was coming head on into the passenger side. I cried out loud, "Oh please don't hit Lola!" And what do you know? She ran right into the passenger's side of my car where my friend Joni was sitting. Oh, what a disaster!

Instead of me taking a left like I heard in my spirit, I did the opposite. Even though I was not at fault in the accident, it left me stranded for hours on the side of the road waiting for a tow truck, dealing with my insurance company, and filling out a police report. Plus, I was in another city two hours from home. My husband had to come and get me that night. I not only put myself in a bad situation, I put my friend Joni and my husband out, too, since they had to make other arrangements as well. Oh, and let's not forget the other drivers who were backed up in traffic from the accident since it was close to five o-clock rush hour traffic. Yep! It was a big mess. I kept saying, "I should have listened. I heard that voice in my spirit saying not to go this way."

Joni reminded me later that the firefighters told us if my car hadn't had reinforced bars, she could have been seriously injured." She believes it was God who kept us safe because it could have been a lot worse.

Now when I hear that small voice, I try my best to settle my thoughts and just be quiet to listen. It's in that still, small voice that I hear and know God's voice. He has something to say, so I pause and listen to that prompting. It's a process of obedience to listen to the voice of God. Ask and you shall receive! So if you don't understand, ask Him questions. Here are a few questions I ask God: "Where do you want to go today, God? What would you have me say to this person, Lord? How do you feel about this situation, Papa God?"

He is listening and will answer, so we must listen. The Holy Spirit always gives the right information that helps us move forward properly. "For those who are led by the Spirit of God are the children of God" (Rom. 8:14).

When I sit down in the mornings to spend time with Papa God, I will often say, "What do you have to say, Lord? I want to hear from You. Teach me something new today." I really do want to hear what He has to say and learn from Him. That's where true wisdom and discernment come from. There are times when I am antsy and can't focus my mind. I don't know about you, but I must battle with my thoughts all the time and try to hold them captive. I must ask myself, "Is it going to be my way or His way?" Just like Elijah had a choice, I have a choice and so do you. Truthfully, I would rather do it His way. "We demolish arguments and every pretension that sets itself up against the knowledge of God, and we take captive every thought to make it obedient to Christ" (2 Cor. 10:5).

Here is the lesson I learned from this situation: I might think my way is better in that moment, and that it may get me there faster. But when I get there, it's typically not the way I had planned. Remember, God has a bird's-eye view of what is ahead. Taking His warnings or commands is for our good. Before you do all this running around, stop and take a minute to pray about what God wants to do and after you ask, say nothing and just listen. His voice sounds like your voice, but it's different in the way it is delivered to your thoughts. Don't try and overthink it. If you do, it is not God. Just stop, listen, and stay silent. A still, small voice will rise in your thoughts, so be ready to hear what He has to say. Believe me; it will change your day!

Once you learn to hear His voice, the next time you hear Him, the situation will go well for you. That is because you will recognize when it's Him speaking and not your own thoughts. To have a relationship with anyone you must have a back and forth conversation. If you and I were in a conversation, and I was the only one speaking all the time, chances are you would become frustrated with me, and we couldn't learn anything from each other. God is no different. God longs to speak to you and for you to hear Him. He loves you and always wants what is best for you.

He's always listening; are you?

Big hugs,
Papa God and Ashley

To Be Born Again?

What do followers of Christ mean when they say they are born again? In John 3:3–4, Nicodemus asked that question of Jesus: "How can a man be born when he is old? Can he enter a second time into his mother's womb and be born?"

We all know that we cannot be born from our mothers again as an adult. For someone who has never heard this before, I am sure Jesus' statement would sound a little odd, knowing that it is impossible. Plus, that would one big baby! Being a mom, I can't even begin to imagine giving birth to a two-hundred-pound baby versus the five- and six-pound babies I had.

As Christians, we know that we cannot inherit salvation unless we accept Jesus as our Lord and Savior. The following verses are great to read regarding this truth: Ezekiel 11:19, Ezekiel 18:31, Ezekiel 36:26, John 1:12–13, John 3:3–7, John 3:18 and 1 Peter 1:3–5.

To be born again means that we are spiritually dead until we ask Jesus into our hearts. A visual example is that of a butterfly. When a caterpillar changes into a beautiful butterfly, it does not act or look like its old self. It is now full of life with brilliant colors. The butterfly becomes an entirely new creation. The old caterpillar self has passed away. The butterfly no longer must crawl to get where it is going. It now has brilliant wings to fly high above the ground.

As Christians and followers of Christ, how does this relate to being born again? First off, if you are a Christian but you are still living like a caterpillar, then it is time to grow and be transformed. That means digging into the Word of God and reading the Bible daily. Don't wait for someone else to teach you. God wants to have a personal relationship with you. Matthew 6:33 says, "But seek first his kingdom and his righteousness, and all these things will be given to you as well." The Holy Spirit is our teacher and advocate. He will teach you to seek God and His ways. His ways are what transforms us to be like Jesus.

The speed of the transformation is different for everyone, but for the most part, things that you used to do before you were a Christian (that came so natural because of a sinful nature) will start to change for the better. The more you desire to learn about God through His written Word, the faster the transformation. Those old habits and desires won't be so important to you anymore. Your life will seem freer, and you will not be bound to the chains that held you to your past.

I recall that when I really got serious about wanting to know God, I couldn't get enough of reading my Bible. It was like a hunger in me that just couldn't be satisfied; I wanted to know more and more. I started to hear God's voice more clearly, and my prophetic dreams increased.

John 8:32 says, "Then you will know the truth, and the truth will set you free." Just like the butterfly that changed and was set free from that old cocoon, it will happen naturally the way God intended it to be. It won't be something you will have to force.

I must mention one important fact about the butterfly. It gains its beautiful colors because its wings press against the cocoon when it pushes its way through to be released. You will make mistakes but keep pressing through for the truth. The reason is because your flesh still wants the same old things from your past, but you must transform your thoughts to the thoughts of God and turn away from the old way of doing things. As it says in Romans 12:2 and Ephesians 4:23, you need to renew, or reprogram, your mind daily. My dad has made this statement, "When you are born again, your spirit man is what instantly changes. Your thoughts and body are not changed in that instant. Your thoughts and actions are in the process of change that can only be altered when you spend time learning from the Holy Spirit."

> Come to me all who are weary and burdened, and I will give you rest. Take my yoke upon you and learn from me, for I am gentle and humble in heart, and you will find rest for your souls. For my yoke is easy and my burden is light. (Matt. 11:28–30)

That picture of the little girl looking at the butterfly from Bonita reminds me of the change that was happening in me. God was first showing me what was happening in the spiritual realm before it happened in the natural realm. Reflecting on this, remember who you are to Him and what He did for us on the cross. He paid the price for us. When we ask Him for forgiveness, in His eyes, we are that changed butterfly. He doesn't see us as who we used to be. He sees us as a new creation in Christ. "Therefore, if anyone is in Christ, the new creation has come: The old has gone, the new is here!" (2 Cor. 5:17).

Break out of that mold from your past self and become who He created you to be. Soar high above the ground into the life you were meant to live.

He *loves* you enough to see you as who you are, not as who you were. Keep your eyes on Him and don't look back. You are no longer who you were; you are born again.

Big hugs,
Papa God and Ashley

Is Good Good Enough?

I want to address an age-old question, and I want to go deeper into what happens to us when we choose Jesus to be our Lord and Savior. I have heard many people ask, "Can we be saved by good works?" They say, "I am a good person, I love my neighbor, and I help the poor, therefore, I think I am going to heaven when I die."

It may be true that you are a good person, but let me ask this question. How good is good? Have you ever talked back to your parents? Well, that's a sin. "Children, obey your parents in the Lord, for this is right" (Eph. 6:1).

Have you ever lied or have you ever taken something from someone else because you had to have it or you needed it? Those are sins. "Do not steal. Do not lie. Do not deceive one another" (Lev. 19:11).

The list goes on and on: cheating, gossiping, and idol worship are among these sins. Anything in our lives we have made more important than God is idolatry. Idolatry is idol worship, and this can include idolizing spouses, children, friends, money, a celebrity, material things (cars, houses, clothes), or even our own selves. Idols are anything that you put before God. You might be saying, "Ouch, Ashley this is brutal!" But what are the first and second commandments in the Ten Commandments? Let's look them up.

> You shall have no other gods before me. You shall not make for yourself an image in the form of anything in heaven above or on the earth beneath or in the waters below. You shall not bow down to them or worship them; for I, the LORD your God, am a jealous God, punishing the children for the sin of the parents to the third and fourth generation of those who hate me, but showing love to a thousand generations of those who love me and keep my commandments. (Ex. 20:3–6)

I can't even begin to tell you how many times in my life I have put others, objects, and myself before my time with God. Put it this way: If I did that to my husband, I wouldn't be married anymore. If Kurt wanted to spend time with me every morning to discuss the plans for the day, and I had something better to do than to talk with him, he wouldn't be very happy with me.

One of the most important things I have ever learned is that God comes first in my life, then my husband, children, church—and everything else comes last. God is a God of order. He designed it that way for a purpose. He will never contradict His order of things. (See Col. 3:18–22.)

In the Old Testament, God gave Moses a set of laws for the Israelites to live by, not so much to put a bunch of rules on them or to punish them, but so that they would be safe, and His people would stand out to others as different people with moral values. The law was a standard so we could be more like God, or as close to Him as we could with our sinful nature; it was something to strive for until Jesus came.

The Ten Commandments (the law of God) teaches us that sin is not acceptable to God because God cannot sin. It is against His life-giving nature or *zoe* life. Zoe, a Greek word, is pronounced dzo-ay. (The d is silent.) I will go into the meaning of zoe life in just a minute. But first

I want to stay on the topic of is good, good enough and build on this foundation. This chapter is full of details so stay with me and really focus on what I am saying to you. I am going to dig into the why and how with the goal of explaining God's purpose and plan for you. Make sure you read this chapter the entire way through. This is not one that you should stop in the middle and go get a bite to eat or answer the phone. You will get lost on what I am saying. OK?

Good. Let's continue.

I am not trying to make you feel bad about yourself, but here is my point to the question: "Are we good enough to make heaven by works alone?" Let's get serious and really ask ourselves, how in the world could we ever measure up (on our own) to the standards God set for us in His commandments? If you need to, go back in your Bible and read the Ten Commandments in Exodus 20.

Romans 3:23 says that we all have sinned and fall short of the glory of God. Because of the fall of Adam, we were all born sinners with his sinful nature. Thank God for His grace and mercy on those who believe, right? Without Jesus as our advocate (someone to stand up for the lost and broken), we would be doomed or damned for eternity because of sin. Without Jesus, there is no way we could keep all the laws and escape a penalty of our sins. We needed a Savior with the life of God in Him and the flesh of fallen man to take the sin of humanity upon Himself for us. "Christ is the culmination of the law so that there may be righteousness for everyone who believes" (Rom. 10:4).

So how is this achieved? How can we sinners stand blameless before a holy God? "For it is by grace you have been saved, through faith—and this is not from yourselves, it is the gift of God—not by works so that no one can boast" (Eph. 2:8–9).

Grace means unmerited favor from God—there is nothing you can do to earn your own way into heaven. It is a free gift from God for those who believe Jesus is His Son, and He died in our place for our trespasses against God. It is a free gift of grace, even when I don't deserve it? I don't know about you, but I'll take that! We can't boast about something we haven't done ourselves. I didn't go hang on the cross and neither did you, nor do either of us want to. I'll admit that I have told lies, and as a child I stole things. Maybe these were small things, but don't fool yourself and say you have never been guilty of these things, too. But thank God for His grace and forgiveness when we repent. That is why Jesus died in our place so that we would give all the credit where credit is due. The law points us to our humanity, and it demonstrates that we were dead in our sins and needed a Savior, and Jesus is the Savior! Ephesians 2:1 says that without Jesus, we would have no hope of heaven or forgiveness of sins.

He was the first human that carried zoe life in Him, God's life. While others were walking around in darkness, He was, and is, the very nature of God Himself; Jesus is God in the flesh.

Because Jesus was and is the only human who never sinned, He paid the price for our sins on the cross as that spotless Lamb, reconciling us to a right standing relationship with God. When you confess Jesus as Lord, your sins are forgiven. There is no other way to God but through Jesus Christ. Scripture says: "If you declare with your mouth, "Jesus is Lord" and believe in your heart that God raised Jesus from the dead, you will be saved. For it is with your heart that you believe and are justified, and it is with your mouth that you profess your faith and are saved" (Rom. 10: 9–10).

You might ask, "That's it?"

Yep! Anyone who trusts Jesus will never be put to shame. As Scripture says, "Anyone who believes in him will never be put to shame" (Rom. 10:11).

Ultimately, it's a heart change and the realization that there isn't anything we could ever do to save ourselves, which in turn changes our minds to think and act more like Jesus. This affects our spirit man to be in unity with the same Spirit of God. When you accept Jesus as your

Lord and Savior, you take on the very zoe life of God. The same life that is in Jesus is now living inside of you.

Zoe life is:

A. Life of the absolute fullness of life, both essential and ethical, which belongs to God, and through Him both to the hypostatic "logos" and Christ in whom the "logos" put on human nature.

B. Life real and genuine, a life active and vigorous, devoted to God, blessed, in the portion even in this world of those who put their trust in Christ, but after the resurrection to be consummated by new accessions (among them a more perfect body), and to last forever.[2]

And logos is:

The Word of God, or principle of divine reason and creative order, identified in the Gospel of John with the second person of the Trinity incarnate in Jesus Christ.

(In Jungian psychology) the principle of reason and judgment, associated with the animus.

Origin:

Greek, "word, reason."[3]

That is a great explanation of what believers carry around inside and a great explanation of the Trinity. Because of our declaration that we believe Jesus is who He said He is, we have the very life of God in us which is *eternal life*. God is eternal, meaning He has existed forever and will live forever. With that said, we are eternal beings as well. We believe

---

2   http://www.biblestudytools.com/lexicons/greek/nas/zoe.html
3   https://www.google.com/search?q=logos&rlz=1C1CHWA_enUS638US639&
oq=logos&aqs=chrome.
0.69i59l2j0l4.4448j0j8&sourceid=chrome&ie=UTF-8#q=logos+definition

this because we live by faith; it is a knowing inside of us that this is the truth even though we have yet to meet Jesus face to face.

Air is a good illustration of God. We can't see air, but we can breathe it, hear it, and feel it. Think about sand and how it blows in the wind and makes rock formations; air even changes the landscape of everything around us, just like the very presence of God changes the internal and external landscape of our lives and the lives of people around us. God is very real even if we cannot see Him with our natural eyes. That is why we have faith and why God sent Jesus as an exact replica of Himself. I invite you to read the following verses to understand more about this topic on your own: Colossians 1:15, 2 Corinthians 4:4, and Hebrews 1:3.

> Fight the good fight of the faith. Take hold of the eternal life to which you were called when you made your good confession in the presence of many witnesses. In the sight of God, who gives life to everything, and of Christ Jesus. (1 Tim. 6:12–13)

> Then they asked him, "What must we do to do the works God requires?" Jesus answered, "The work of God is this: to believe in the one he has sent." (John 6:28–29)

To tie this all together, I want to share an experience I had to help you understand what I am saying on a more personal level. One weekend, I went to a Christian concert in a park. I was asked to be at this concert as an advocate promoting Holt International Children's Services. Along with other vendors, I had a table set up with picture cards of the Holt children, asking for sponsors.

Just before I left the event, I saw that two other vendors were having a hard time breaking down their tent. A tent peg was stuck, and the ladies needed help and the understanding of how to repair the broken peg. When I noticed their difficulty in collapsing the tent, I had said a prayer out loud and asked God to help them. Both ladies agreed to my prayer with an, "Amen." Not even a second later, I turned my head, and a man was walking by us on the sidewalk. I made eye contact with him, and I asked if he was handy.

He said, "Yes I am." He walked over to us, and we briefly told him the issue and asked if he wouldn't mind helping them collapse their tent. Much to our surprise, God provided what we needed right away. We were all excited because he figured out the issue. I proceeded to tell this nice man that I had just asked God to help these ladies, and he had just so happened to walk up at that very moment as the answer to our prayer.

As you can imagine, this comment started a conversation about God. We introduced ourselves to each other, and he told me that his name was Carlos. Carlos explained that he was homeless, and that he had gone to church when he was a boy, but he was afraid to get close to God because he was "a runner." Doesn't this sound like a familiar story? I knew right away in my spirit that Carlos was a prodigal.

In other words, he was afraid of God because he had sin in his life and had made bad choices along the way. He continued telling me that he had not been to church in a long time. I could tell that he wasn't sure of his salvation. I told Carlos about the story of the Prodigal Son, and how the father was waiting on the hill for his son to return home. I explained how the Prodigal Son had wasted his life, and the father forgave him even though he had sinned. We discussed how God has plans to use Carlos for His good purpose in the earth.

As I unfolded the story of the Prodigal Son to Carlos, tears filled his eyes. He looked at me and said, "I want to know God like that, Ashley." So I asked him if I could pray with him and we said the prayer of salvation together. It was in that moment that he dedicated his life to Christ.

The next thing Carlos said to me made my heart melt: "You don't know what you have just done for me. No one has ever prayed with me like that." I gave him a big hug and introduced him to a few other people from in his area who could lead him to church and keep him on the new path set before him.

I felt good about what I had just experienced, but you know what touched my heart the most? Carlos was a really nice guy; he did a good thing to help us, and he genuinely wanted to know that God loved him. I did find it sad, though, that Carlos was possibly in his early thirties, but no one had ever prayed for him like he said I did. It concerned me to know that he went to church as a child but had never received Jesus as His Lord and Savior; this was sad to hear.

Listen, I am not tooting my own horn. I make mistakes all the time, and this experience was an awakening for me. I started praying, "God, where is the church?" We can't wait for these people to come into our churches searching for God. Jesus went out into the city streets and taught the people. He dedicated His life to finding the lost to bring them home and shined His light in the darkness.

Knowing this to be true, I understand that there is a reason why God appointed different positions in the body of Christ. (See 1 Cor. 12, Rom. 12:6–8.) Ephesians 4:11–13 says God has given abilities and gifts to each of us so that we can fulfill His purposes in the earth through Christ. Know, reader, that we will be held accountable for using our gifts and talents or not when we stand before God on judgment day. So it is important to God that we do good works, but we must understand that good works are not what will get us into heaven. "For we must all appear before the judgment seat of Christ, so that each of us may receive what is due us for the things done while in the body, whether good or bad" (2 Cor. 5:10).

Carlos was in the dark and so badly wanted someone to tell him about the love of Jesus and that God has great plans for him. I truly believe he blindly hoped he was going to heaven because he went to church when he was a boy. He had made some bad choices in life, but he was still a good person. Yet he was lost spiritually and confused about his salvation. He was a sinner, but God wanted Carlos to know he is forgiven, and that He wanted him to come home to God. Even though Carlos was a good person and was willing to help three women break down their tables and tents, he was spiritually dead inside and didn't even know it.

He was kind because God is kind, and God created us, but that doesn't mean Carlos was going to heaven when he died. He didn't have zoe life or eternal life in him yet. (Adam handed that over to Satan in the garden when he sinned against God.) Carlos had to confess Jesus as Lord first, and his eyes had to be opened to the truth of God. This can only be done through the prompting and leading of the Holy Spirit. (See John 16:13–15.)

After the event, I realized the other reason I was there that day. It was not only to spread the word about the orphans under Holt International's care; the divine purpose of being there was that I brought the light that was in me—zoe life or everlasting life—and the love of God for His people.

Looking at this from another angle, just because I am a pastor's daughter and a Christian doesn't mean that my faith will get my children into heaven when they pass on into glory. They must have their own relationship with God directly. Our credentials and background do not save us. We are saved by faith in Jesus Christ and the grace of God based on what Christ did for us on the cross.

Unlike Carlos, let's suppose someone has gone to church their whole life but has never confessed Jesus as their Lord and Savior. Do they enter heaven when they pass away? I hate to be the bearer of bad news but the answer is no. Here is an example the Holy Spirit gave me to share with you. Let's imagine a single young man who is a great guy and comes from a wonderful family, and he comes into my home as a guest. During this visit, he takes notice of one of my daughters, and he thinks she is beautiful. They both like each other a lot by appearance and he comes over every weekend to see her, but there is no exchange of meaningful words with each other and no true relationship is ever formed.

Then one day my daughter and I go out shopping, and someone comes up to congratulate her on her marriage to this nice young man. But my daughter is still single, so we think it's a joke and dismiss it. Then I hear from others that this young man is running around telling everyone that he and my daughter are married. This would be very confusing and frustrating because there has never been a wedding nor has there ever really been a relationship between the two. This is absurd because everyone knows that they must be in a relationship first (a coming together in agreement), and then he is to ask her and seek her father's permission to marry before the ceremony takes place. Let's not forget there must be witnesses at the ceremony as well to confirm the union.

Now let's say that the two do fall in love, and they exchange wedding vows; my daughter will leave with her groom, and they start a loving life together in their own home. Scripture is very clear on this. Jesus is the Bridegroom waiting for His bride, and God is not looking at what we have done ourselves because we cannot save ourselves, and we can't enter heaven without the Bridegroom just like we can't marry ourselves. It takes two to have a union, and Jesus is the only way to God in heaven. Jesus answered, "I am the way and the truth and the life. No one comes to the Father except through me" (John 14:6).

If we could save ourselves, Jesus died for nothing. To be saved, we must individually come together in unity with God with this understanding, *confess* it with our mouths, and *believe* that Jesus is the Son of God. Just because Carlos went to church didn't mean he asked Jesus into his heart. He only visited the church and then, like many, he ran from the church. In the park that day, he came to this understanding and confessed Jesus as his Lord and Savior.

Maybe you're reading this and thinking, "I know I am a sinner, and yet I'm good person. Now I understand that being good just isn't enough." If you have come to recognize this truth, I pray that you get real with God right now where you are. Surrendering your heart is where this starts and on then bended knees, bow your head to dedicate or rededicate your life back to Him.

Don't let the enemy make you think you've got this on your own or that you have run too far for God to forgive you. That is not true! That is a lie from Satan to stop you from surrendering your life to the Lord. God loves you. Remember, Jesus already paid the price for your sins, but it is up to you to ask Him to be Lord and Savior.

It is that simple. All you must do is ask. God *will* hear you and respond with love, mercy, and grace. God is not a man who would lie. It's against His nature to lie. He wants to give you His nature, zoe life. "God is not human, that he should lie, not a human being, that he should change his mind. Does he speak and then not act? Does he promise and not fulfill?" (Num. 23:19).

When God makes a promise, He keeps it, and when we ask, God acts immediately. If this is touching your heart, God is waiting on that hill for you to come home. Can you see it? If this is you, don't walk; run into the arms of Jesus and never look back to the things behind you. You don't live there anymore because you are forgiven by Papa God.

Prayer: God, I know that I am sinner, and that being a good person isn't enough to bring me into a right relationship with You. I have put others and things before my relationship with You. At times, I even thought I could save myself and enter heaven on my own merit. Because of this mindset, I have run so far from You, but because of Your grace, I am ready to come home. I know You have great plans for me and because of Your love for me, I want to be in a relationship with Your Son Jesus. Let it be recorded in the Lamb's Book of Life that today I asked You, Jesus, to be my Lord and Savior. God, I want You to be my number One, and I ask You to forgive me and to transform me into a new creation. I ask You for zoe life in Jesus. Amen.

Now you can walk into heaven together with Christ one day by His work not your own. But this is only the beginning. You and Papa God have some work to do together!

Big hugs,
Papa God and Ashley

Last Minute Hal

As I have mentioned previously, my dad is a pastor at Word of Life Church in Apopka, Florida. As part of his ministry, hospital visits to his congregation members are a part of his calling. The word *pastor* derives from Scripture, meaning someone who leads their flock; this flock is God's sheep. Mark 10:44, John 21:16, Acts 6:1–6, Acts 20:17, and 1 Peter 5:1–2 are just a handful of Scriptures in the New Testament that record what a pastor is called to do as the leader of the church. "Again Jesus said, 'Simon son of John, do you love me?' He answered, 'Yes, Lord, you know that I love you.' Jesus said, 'Take care of my sheep.'" (John 21:16).

In other words, pastors are responsible for shepherding the people in their church body. Their main responsibilities are to feed them the Word of God, comfort the members in their time of need, protect them from the enemy, and correct them with Scripture when necessary. Their ultimate goal is to teach the members of the church body how to go out into the world and preach the good news of Jesus Christ, heal the sick, and set the captives free through the gifts and talents given them by God. For more research on this topic see Ephesians 4:11 and 1 Corinthians 12:1–11.

It can be challenging to teach someone in crisis who has not been fed the Word of God consistently. It is difficult for a pastor when they don't know the one in crisis on a personal level. It's like trying to tell someone something in a thirty-minute window of time what they should have been learning over years, weeks, and days of their lives with their pastor, who leads them every step of the way. It doesn't mean it can't happen. It's just more of a challenge for the pastor and for the person to understand the big picture; they only get a glimpse of what Jesus did for them.

That is why it is imperative to find a good church family that can mentor you throughout your journey of life. It is so nice to know that God designed us to have godly leaders who care for us and help us when we need them, always directing us back to the Word of God. If they know that person on a more personal level, it is easy to connect with them on what God says because there is an established, trusting bond.

One of the members of my dad's church is a lady named Teresa. She approached my dad with great concern because her father was in the hospital dying of cancer. Typically, my dad doesn't visit people in the hospital who are not a part of his church body for the reasons previously disclosed. However, because Teresa had great concern for her father's life, my dad decided to go visit him. Prior to his visit, Teresa mentioned that she didn't believe her dad was born again. She informed my dad that over the years, multiple attempts had been made to lead her father to the Lord but were without success. The sense of urgency was great due to his health, so my dad decided to visit her father a few days later in the hospital.

On the way to the hospital, my dad started praying. He said, "Lord, open this man's eyes and his heart so that he will hear, see, and understand the gospel." My dad then bound the devil and took authority over Satan to keep him from interfering in any way, removing that obstacle.

When my dad arrived at the hospital, he walked into Hal's room. Straightaway, my dad could sense the feelings of hopelessness in Hal because he said it was written all over his face. My dad introduced himself as Pastor Darrell Morgan, and said that his daughter, Teresa, had asked him to come visit.

Hal looked up at my dad and said, "Pastor, thank you for coming."

In my dad's famous style, he kindly jumped right to the purpose of his visit. "Hal, do you know the Lord? Are you a Christian?"

Hal replied, "No pastor, I do not know the Lord, and I am not a Christian. I have had many people tell me about Jesus, but I just don't believe."

My dad said, "What is it that you don't believe?"

Then Hal explained all that he believed and didn't believe based on his experiences and understanding throughout his life. Finally, the truth came out of the bag, and Hal confessed that he just didn't understand the truth behind his unbelief. He said, "Pastor, I just don't understand."

Let us reflect on the point when my dad entered the room and focus our attention on that feeling of hopelessness he could sense in Hal. My dad passionately explained the story like this: "Hal is lying on this death bed in the hospital. He knows his time is short, and he also knows that he is a sinner. When he dies he is going to hell, and in his mind, there is nothing he can do about it. That is because he has never had anyone explain the gospel to him correctly." The Scripture he used to back up his assessment is found in the book of Ephesians. "Remember that at that time you were separate from Christ, excluded from citizenship in Israel and foreigners to the covenants of the promise, without hope and without God in the world" (Eph. 2:12).

This Scripture clarifies the hopelessness for those in the world without Jesus as their Lord and Savior. My dad explained, "To too many people, that's a big deal. They realize they have sinned and have fallen short of the glory of God. As far as they are concerned there is nothing they can do about it. And in their minds, they are correct."

Knowing this, my dad looked at Hal and responded to him by pointing out his hopelessness and lack of understanding. He wanted Hal to know that there is hope in Jesus. He said, "Hal, thirty minutes from now your name will be written in the Lamb's Book of Life."

With a sense of peace and appreciation, Hal responded, "You know what? I really hope so."

My dad could relate to Hal's lack of understanding. It was in that response that my dad knew how he could help Hal. He said, "Hal, I have been a pastor for forty years, and I still don't understand. The Bible doesn't say, 'To those who understand . . .' There are a lot of things I don't understand. I don't know how Jesus died and rose from the dead exactly, but I believe it."

That is when the Holy Spirit prompted my dad to turn to John 3:16, and he read it to Hal and then continued through verse 18.

For God so loved the world that he gave his one and only Son, that whoever believes in him shall not perish but have eternal life. For God did not send his Son into the world to condemn the world, but to save the world through him. Whoever believes in him is not condemned, but whoever does not believe stands condemned already because they have not believed in the name of God's one and only Son. (John 3:16–18)

After reading this to Hal, my dad looked up at him and said, "Hal, do you understand that people do not go to hell for sinning?" Hal looked at my dad with a perplexed expression on his face and told him he had never heard that statement before in his entire life.

So my dad, seeing his confusion, read the Scripture one more time because he really wanted him to grasp the meaning of what is written in the Word of God. With that said, let's go over the Scripture again, but I am going to emphasize the words I want us to reflect on.

> For God so loved the world that he gave his one and only Son, that whoever believes in him shall not perish but have eternal life. For God did not send his Son into the world to condemn the world, but to save the world through him. *Whoever believes in him is not condemned, but whoever does not believe stands condemned already because they have not believed in the name of God's one and only Son.* (John 3:16–18 emphasis added)

My dad continued the conversation with Hal and made this statement, "Jesus took your place on the cross and died for you. Jesus did that in your place so that you don't have to die for your own sin. The only thing separating you from God is your rejection of Jesus."

When my dad said this to him, he could see Hal's eyes light up with this new revelation. My dad explained to him, "All the things that you have done wrong, we all have done, and we all have fallen short of the glory of God. This is what has you hung up, Hal. You are looking at all the things you have done wrong, and you know that you can't stand before God." He continued, "Jesus did it for you." Then my dad opened his Bible to Romans 10:9–10 and asked Hal to read the Scripture. He handed Hal the Bible and said, "I want you to read it out loud." So Hal took the Bible and read:

> If you declare with your mouth, "Jesus is Lord," and believe in your heart that God raised him from the dead, you will be saved. For it is with your heart that you believe and are justified, and it is with your mouth that you profess your faith and are saved. (Rom. 10:9–10)

And he continued into verse 11:

As Scripture says, "Anyone who believes in him will never be put to shame." (Rom. 10:11)

My dad then asked Hal, "Do you believe that Jesus died on the cross for you?"

Hal said, "Yes I do."

My dad replied, "The Bible says that if you believe in what He did and you confess Him as Lord, you will be born again."

I love this part of the story because Hal comes alive with excitement, and my dad said that Hal looked at him with the biggest smile on his face like, "Are you serious?"

Just then, Hal grabbed my dad's hands and squeezed them boldly with delight. Right then and there, Hal started praying, "Oh God, I do believe that Jesus died for me, I do believe that Jesus rose from the dead. I do believe! And I ask you to come into my heart! I want You to be the Lord of my life!" My dad said that once Hal said these words, his face lit up like a neon sign. With tears rolling down his face, Hal started to cry.

This touched my dad's heart and he said, "As of now, everything you have ever done wrong in the past is gone. You are a new creation, and you have been made righteous in Christ Jesus. If you died right now, you would go straight to heaven because of Jesus."

My dad said that as he walked out of that hospital room, he saw Hal with his hands in the air and worshiping God. Hallelujah! My dad was so happy for Hal because he said that, "What started off as a hopeless day, ended as a day of good news." My dad continued, "Today the gospel has not been preached in America like it should be preached. People do not understand what Jesus did." I believe that is why the Holy Spirit prompted me to write this book. When I heard my dad tell this story, I just knew it needed to be included.

The first thing that I want you to take away from this story is how to lead someone to the Lord. But I also want you to know why most people say no to going to church or surrendering their hearts to the Lord. When my dad asked Hal why he didn't believe, he finally admitted that it was because he didn't understand. The issue wasn't that he didn't want to understand, he simply just didn't understand. Maybe the sermons he heard in the past didn't touch his heart and there was never a breakthrough in his way of thinking. I am sure it was also because of his focus on his sins, and that he felt he couldn't go to church, leading him to believe he couldn't approach a holy God. This is a common misconception and a lie from Satan that sends these people to eternal punishment for rejecting Jesus.

Another key factor to recognize is that my dad handed the Bible to Hal, and had Hal read the Scripture for himself. There is life in the Word of God, and the Word is what changes our hearts and opens our eyes to the truth. My dad wasn't just telling Hal how to be saved; Hal read it himself. This is very important when leading someone to the Lord or showing them something in Scripture.

My dad also taught me something helpful for leading people to the Lord and beyond. After the prayer of salvation, I often buy them a Bible or ask them if they already have one. The reason is that I don't just want to lead them to the cross and then let them off on their own to try and survive. I want to mentor them on their journey.

I ask if I can highlight Scriptures pertaining to specific topics for them. For salvation, for instance, I use a specific color to highlight the Scriptures. Then in pen, I write the Scripture reference in the front of their Bible and specify the color highlighter I used. This way it is easy for them to access specific Scriptures with that topic. For example, when they have their Bible in hand, they look to the front of the book where I wrote the Scriptures. As they turn the pages, they may see pink highlighted Scriptures on salvation. If you're feeling really ambitious, you can go a little further and use another color like a yellow highlighter for the Holy Spirit, orange for healing, and green for prosperity Scriptures. You choose the colors you feel are best; these are just examples for a starting point. Later, when I present the Bible to them, I show them where I wrote the Scripture reference in the front of their Bibles and then take them to the Scriptures. Since the Scriptures are highlighted in that same color, it's easy because their eyes go directly to the highlighted verse.

Recalling the chapter called, "Tie Your Shoelaces," you can teach them about the Old Testament (the old agreement between God and man) and the New Testament (the new agreement between God and man). Simply explain that everything from the Old Testament points to the first coming of Jesus and the New Testament is the fulfillment of the Old Testament through Jesus. This helps them understand why we read both Old and New together.

Here are some of the salvation Scriptures I have in my own Bible. Having these Scriptures already highlighted helps me to flip right to them when I am in the process of leading someone to the Lord.

Romans 3:21–22, 4:25–5:1, 10:9–11
Ephesians 2:8–9
John 3:16–18, 6:29
Acts 4:10–12
1 John 5:11–13

Like my dad did for Hal, when leading someone to the Lord, I like to start with John 3:16 and follow up with Romans 10:9–11. This seems to be the best way for me to show them the salvation message quickly and understandably.

Dad told me that Hal did end up going home to be with the Lord. He had a little more time with Hal to comfort him and direct him in prayer. We celebrate his life and his daughter Teresa for the urgency to help her father. Even though Hal waited until the last minute, he was still able to enter into the gates of heaven. This is not something I would recommend because we never know when our last breath will be. But God knew He could use someone like my dad to tell Hal how much God loves him, and that Hal still had a chance to give his heart to Jesus by accepting Him as his Lord and Savior.

I hope this story encourages you to lead people to the Lord. Keep in mind, I believe that most people really do want to surrender their lives to the Lord, but they just don't understand how and why they need to. "And how can anyone preach unless they are sent? As it is written: 'How beautiful are the feet of those who bring good news!'" (Rom. 10:15).

The most important takeaway here is that God loves us, and the only way to the Father is through Jesus Christ. There is no other way. We can't save ourselves, and the good news is that Jesus did it all for us so we wouldn't have to. In a world full of hopelessness, it is imperative to tell others that there is hope in Jesus. Their eternity depends on it.

Big hugs,
Papa God and Ashley

Engrafted into Christ

So we have learned about zoe life, logos, and how asking Jesus to be our Lord and Savior is asking the Spirit of God to come live inside us. As if that wasn't deep enough, have you ever wondered why Christians aren't considered Jewish? Jesus was Jewish, and we believe that Jesus is God in the flesh. Did God reject the Jewish people because some of them did not recognize Jesus as the promised Messiah when He walked this earth? There were several hundred prophecies in the Old Testament that Jesus fulfilled to the letter to prove that He is who He says He is. It has been proven that Jesus fulfilled around 353 prophecies.

Isaiah 53 (Old Testament) is a really good prophecy to read. It goes over in detail what would happen at the crucifixion, so it baffles me why more Jewish people can't see this.

What makes Christians different from Jewish people? Does God love one more than the other? I have even heard someone say that all Jewish people will go to heaven because of the covenant God made with Abraham. If this is the case, then why would they even need a Savior, and why in the world would the Jewish people want to crucify their promised Messiah for claiming to be God in the flesh? (See John 10:30–33, John 18:28–38.)

I've pondered these questions myself and have searched the Word of God for the answers. One morning as I was spending time with Papa God, the Holy Spirit led me to Romans 11. In this chapter, the apostle Paul is writing to the Gentile Christians (non-Jews) about being engrafted into the body of Christ. Let's read what Paul said.

> The Remnant of Israel
> I ask then: Did God reject his people? By no means! I am an Israelite myself, a descendant of Abraham, from the tribe of Benjamin. God did not reject his people, whom he foreknew. Don't you know what Scripture says in the passage about Elijah—how he appealed to God against Israel: "Lord, they have killed your prophets and torn down your altars; I am the only one left, and they are trying to kill me"? (Rom. 11:1–3)

Paul was a Christian Jew, a Christ-follower who happened to be of Jewish descent. This Scripture tells us that God did not forget His covenant with the Jewish people, but I thank God that He didn't turn His back on all mankind as well. In 2 Timothy 1:11, Paul writes that he was appointed to preach the Word of God to the Gentiles. This tells me that Jesus came to save everyone: Jews and non-Jews.

Because Jesus died for all, when we accept Jesus as Lord and Savior, we become united with Christ, part of the body of Christ with Jesus being the head. We are then engrafted into the family of God. "I am the vine; you are the branches. If you remain in me and I in you, you will bear much fruit; apart from me you can do nothing. If you do not remain in me, you are like a branch that is thrown away and withers; such branches are picked up, thrown into the fire and burned" (John 15:5–6).

We need the vine to be able to produce the fruit of God in our lives. Apart from the Vine, we are fruitless, dried up, and cut off—spiritually dead and cast into the fire.

The word *engrafted* means to unite a shoot or bud with a growing plant by insertion or by placing in close contact, to join (a plant or plants) by such union.

One day, my friend Nicky and I were talking about what makes Christians different from the Jewish people. I started telling her what the Lord had shown me about being engrafted.

She was trying to fully understand what exactly that meant as a Christ-follower. The Holy Spirit gave me a visual, and I thought of a farmer who wanted to have a two-colored apple: part red and part green.

The farmer took the stem of a red apple and a stem of a green apple and twisted them together. After several months of watering and tending to the plant, it produced a hybrid apple that was both red and green. This apple became a new creation, something that was not ever seen before, and now it was a new kind of fruit.

Nicky said, "Ashley, that's a great visual to give a better perspective on how two great things can combine into one!"

I love how *The Message* Bible paraphrases the combining of the two groups of people, Jewish and non-Jewish.

The Messiah has made things up between us so that we're now together on this, both non-Jewish outsiders and Jewish insiders. He tore down the wall we used to keep each other at a distance. He repealed the law code that had become so clogged with fine print and footnotes that it hindered more than it helped. Then he started over. Instead of continuing with two groups of people separated by centuries of animosity and suspicion, he created a new kind of human being, a fresh start for everybody. Christ brought us together through his death on the cross. The Cross got us to embrace, and that was the end of the hostility. Christ came and preached peace to you outsiders and peace to us insiders. He treated us as equals, and so made us equals. Through him we both share the same Spirit and have equal access to the Father. (Eph. 2:14–18 MSG)

The New International Version of the Bible puts it this way:

For he himself is our peace, who has made the two groups one and has destroyed the barrier, the dividing wall of hostility, by setting aside in his flesh the law with its commands and regulations. His purpose was to create in himself one new humanity out of the two, thus making peace, and in one body to reconcile both of them to God through the cross, by which he put to death their hostility. He came and preached peace to you who were far away and peace to those who were near. For through him we both have access to the Father by one Spirit. (Eph. 2:14–18)

When Nicky and I hung up the phone, I asked the Holy Spirit to reveal more to me about this. He showed me that because of the covenant God made with Abraham, the Jewish people had a covenant under the Law of Moses. But because the law could never be achieved by mankind due to sin, God sent Jesus, a descendant of Abraham, to fulfill the law. "For the law was given through Moses; grace and truth came through Jesus Christ" (John 1:17).

Then the Holy Spirit led me to Matthew 5:17 where Jesus was talking about Himself regarding the fulfillment of the Law. From the beginning, God knew that someone with a sinless life would be used as a sacrifice on our behalf. Being full of sin ourselves, Lord knows we would have not been allowed to be nailed to a cross to save humanity! It had to be God who came down to live in and among us as a descendant of Adam, the original man, the earthly father of all humans.

God is the law of justice and mercy, so we can't abolish the laws or standards He asks us to live by. If that were so, we would live in lawlessness and everything would be out of control and chaotic. Jesus did not sin, and yet he did not come to take away the law; He came to make the law complete in Himself.

The Fulfillment of the Law
Do not think that I have come to abolish the Law or the Prophets; I have not come to abolish them but to fulfill them. (Matt. 5:17)

The apostle Paul said it like this to the church in Rome:

Life through the Spirit
Therefore, there is now no condemnation for those who are in Christ Jesus, because through Christ Jesus the law of the Spirit who gives life has set you free from the law of sin and death. For what the law was powerless to do because it was weakened by the flesh, God did by sending his own Son in the likeness of sinful flesh to be a sin offering. And so he condemned sin in the flesh, in order that the righteous requirement of the law might be fully met in us, who do not live according to the flesh but according to the Spirit. (Rom. 8:1–4)

Through Jesus, the sin of all mankind was placed on Himself, fulfilling the law for us. Think about that for a second—*all* of mankind. That includes the sins of people like Hitler, Joseph Stalin, and even someone like Ted Bundy, a serial killer in the 1970s. We assume that these men were condemned to eternal death and hell because of their horrible sins and disconnection to Jesus. Hopefully, they had the chance to confess their sins and repent before they died. We won't know if that is true until we enter heaven ourselves and see if they did or not. My point in mentioning these men is that their sins were placed on the body of Jesus on the cross. That is only a few of many in this world who have done the worst of sins. Think about all the people who have lived and who are yet to be born. That's a whole lot of sin, isn't it?

According to the Merriam-Webster dictionary, the word *condemned* means:

A: to pronounce guilty: <u>convict</u>

B: <u>sentence</u>, <u>doom,</u> condemn a prisoner to die.[4]

The law was made perfect through the sacrifice and blood of Jesus to reconnect us to the vine, Jesus. We no longer live by our flesh, we now live by the Spirit of God. Do you recall when God breathed His breath into Adam? Adam experienced death when he sinned and was separated from God spiritually. He was doomed and condemned to eternal death. We were all doomed under Adam until Jesus reconciled us to God. (See Rom. 5:12–21.)

This is amazing considering God knew no one other than Jesus could ever be perfect. It is by the grace of God that we are saved from sin and death. Believers in Jesus Christ are now made alive spiritually, no longer condemned or damned to a place called hell. Praise God! That should make us want to jump and do back flips for what Jesus did for us. Jesus never sinned, but God knew we needed a Savior who was spotless of sin. Jesus was the Lamb to be slain fulfilling the covenant promise through Abraham. "God made him who had no sin to be sin for us, so that in him we might become the righteousness of God" (2 Cor. 5:21).

I started thinking to myself, "OK, this is great, but there has to be more to all of this. How is Jesus the Lord of all humanity?" For more Scriptures on this, look up Jeremiah 32:27, Acts 17:24–28, and 1 Corinthians 8:6.

We learned that Jesus is God in the flesh. (See Lev. 26:12, John 8:58, Col. 2:9.) There had to be more to the flesh side of the story of Jesus and how He could take back humanity and make us in right standing with God. Then the Holy Spirit started to show me the genealogy of Jesus so that we can see why Jews and Gentiles (non-Jews) can both

---

4   https://www.merriam-webster.com/dictionary/condemned

be engrafted into the vine. This is what the prophet Isaiah said of the coming Messiah. Keep in mind, Isaiah lived approximately 700 years before Christ. He declared that Jesus would be an offspring of Jesse who was King David's father.

The Branch from Jesse
A shoot will come up from the stump of Jesse; from his roots a Branch will bear fruit. The Spirit of the Lord will rest on him—the Spirit of wisdom and of understanding, the Spirit of counsel and of might, the Spirit of the knowledge and fear of the Lord—and he will delight in the fear of the Lord. He will not judge by what he sees with his eyes, or decide by what he hears with his ears; but with righteousness he will judge the needy, with justice he will give decisions for the poor of the earth. He will strike the earth with the rod of his mouth; with the breath of his lips he will slay the wicked. Righteousness will be his belt and faithfulness the sash around his waist. (Isa. 11:1–5)

Remember when Jesus said in John 15:5, "I am the vine and you are the branches"? This Scripture correlates to Isaiah 11:1, predicting that Jesus would be a "shoot that would come up from the stump of Jesse; from his roots, a Branch will bear fruit." This root of Jesse, this branch who will rise up is Jesus! Do you see that?

When I read this, it blew my mind. Now I am going to blow your mind even more. I hope you are ready! I am giving you a little homework, but I promise it will be worth the research. The Holy Spirit led me to even more about the genealogy of Jesus. I can't wait for you to see this!

Please look up Luke 3:21–37 and Matthew 1:1–17. I want you to read this for yourself. I don't want you to just take my word for it. Look and see what God says about Jesus; look at the lineage through the bloodline of Jesse and King David. This is the historically documented proof of who Jesus is.

Grab your Bible and compare the genealogies against each other. Let's start in Matthew 1:1–17. This is Joseph's side of the genealogy, even though Joseph was not Jesus' biological father, God is. Joseph adopted Jesus as his son. I love telling that to kids who have been adopted and how God will not leave them as orphans. Joseph must have been a pretty awesome guy! (See John 14:18.) It was customary for the genealogy to be given for both parents at that time. Do you recall when Joseph and Mary went together to give a census of their genealogies? You can go back and read it in Luke 2:1. Joseph's side gives a clear genealogy of Jesus from David and Abraham.

Luke 3:21–37, however, traces the genealogy back to Adam and down the line to the virgin Mary, emphasizing that Jesus is the Savior for *all* since we all came from Adam. *Wow!* I hope you are looking this up and get this because it only gets better from there! The marvelous part of all of this is that Luke was a doctor, and doctors are researchers and known to keep precise records. Doctors need to know the truth, and accurate documentation is critical in their line of work.

The reason why Matthew and Luke listed the genealogy of Jesus separately is because it shows that both Mary and Joseph were related to Abraham, Jesse, and King David. Their genealogies merged at King David, and the divide happened in David's sons: Nathan who was on Mary's side and King Solomon who was on Joseph's side, accounting for Jesus as the rightful heir to the throne. Another important observation is that on Mary's side of the genealogy, Luke documents her bloodline as not only going all the way back to Adam, but ending (or beginning) at God. This is solid evidence that Jesus is the true Messiah who is the promised Savior and the Lord of *all*. As Scripture says, "Anyone who believes in him will never be put to shame. For there is no difference between Jew and Gentile—the same Lord is Lord of all and richly blesses all who call on him" (Rom. 10:11–12).

Here is where it gets even better. When we ask Jesus to be our Lord and Savior, we become co-heirs with Christ. We are now sons and daughters of the King of all kings. We were adopted into the family of God!

> For those who are led by the Spirit of God are the children of God. The Spirit you received does not make you slaves, so that you live in fear again; rather, the Spirit you received brought about your *adoption* to sonship. And by him we cry, "*Abba*, Father." The Spirit himself testifies with our spirit that we are God's children. Now if we are children, then we are heirs—heirs of God and co-heirs with Christ, if indeed we share in his sufferings in order that we may also share in his glory. (Rom. 8:14–17 emphasis added)

That revelation should make your heart leap for joy! All humanity, Jewish or non-Jewish, should want to be connected to Jesus, to be combined into one body of Christ. I know we all want to be blessed and live a great life. God hasn't left any of us to be orphaned. We are all able to be adopted into His family through His Son.

Most of us want to be able to help others and share the abundant fruit God gives us, fruit that will last forever. Once we see who Jesus really is, we should all want to tap into the nourishment of the Vine only Jesus can give us. Did you notice the end of that Scripture in Romans 10:11–12? It says, "He blesses all who call on Him." As family members of God and co-heirs of His Son, Jesus Christ, we are blessed! We are in God's will. Whatever belongs to God now belongs to His children. Wrap your thoughts around that statement. What have you inherited through the sonship?

> Jesus answered, "I am the way and the truth and the life. No one comes to the Father except through me. If you really know me, you

will know my Father as well. From now on, you do know him and have seen him." (John 14:6–7)

Believe me when I say that I am in the Father and the Father is in me; or at least believe on the evidence of the works themselves. Very truly I tell you, whoever believes in me will do the works I have been doing, and they will do even greater things than these because I am going to the Father. And I will do whatever you ask in my name, so that the Father may be glorified in the Son. You may ask me for anything in my name, and I will do it. (John 14:11–14)

God has not rejected anyone who wants to be connected to the Vine. He sent Jesus to us because He loves us. Anyone who wants to bear fruit must stay connected to God through Jesus Christ, as Jesus is the only way to God.

Once we are a part of the Vine, Jesus said we will do even greater things than He did. One of the ways to do this is bring others by the multitudes to repentance through the cross. We do this though our own story of salvation. God wants to use your story to set others free. Your story has a purpose for the kingdom of God, so don't hide it, tell it. There will be others who find your story relatable to theirs.

The second way is through love. Jesus gave a command to love one another and to bring others with you into heaven. God created you and me because He wanted a family. This is why I call God, Papa. I belong to Him, and He belongs to me. We have a relationship as Papa and daughter. These are the greater things Jesus was talking about.

To do greater things than Jesus did, our spirit man—the eternal part of our three-part makeup: spirit, mind, and body—needs to stay in constant contact with the Vine. This is the relationship. The mind is renewed to the Word of God, and the body surrenders to the obedience of Christ. (See Rom. 12:1–2.) Though you are born again and your spirit is alive unto God, your soul must be renewed—your mind, your will, and your emotions—and your body He said to put it under or to keep it under. How cool it is that if we accept Jesus as Lord and spend time with God, we are engrafted into Him? If we want to know something, all we must do is ask, and the Holy Spirit will always reveal it to us. His very words will keep us not only well nourished, but produce a lot of good fruit.

When we are spiritually filled, we become happy, healthy, and are better equipped for helping others so that they, too, can become a part of the Vine. God is good. He doesn't want anyone to perish, but He wants us to come to repentance. (See 2 Peter 3:9.)

I have been asked over and over by people who question if hell is a real place. They say, "If God is so good, then how could He send people to hell?" Did you know that God doesn't send anyone to hell for being a bad person? God is good, and His ways are morally perfect. (See Ps. 18:30.) God sends people to hell for the rejection of and rebellion against Jesus and the dismissal of a relationship with Him. (See Matt. 25:41, Rom. 6:23.) Because God knows no sin, hell is where God is not, and the just punishment is eternal disconnection from Jesus, the Vine. Apart from the Vine is the eternal punishment of death for the condemned prisoner. "He will reply, 'Truly I tell you, whatever you did not do for one of the least of these, you did not do for me.' Then they will go away to eternal punishment, but the righteous to eternal life" (Matt. 25:45–46).

The righteous ones (in right standing with God) have zoe life (eternal life) with God.

I assume this mention of hell has some a little frightened and some wanting to learn more. I encourage you to study the Scriptures on heaven and hell on your own. I can imagine that this chapter is a little overwhelming because it is full of details of which you are now curious. Seriously, you could probably spend hours upon hours researching all about the lineage of Jesus, the Vine, zoe life, heaven, and hell.

With that said, I will end this chapter with a suggestion of a book for you to read: *23 Minutes in Hell* by Bill Wiese. God doesn't want anyone going to this place, and it is imperative that you understand that hell exists just as heaven is very real as well. This book is eye-opening, but I didn't feel it was scary when I read it. I truly felt that it was vitally freeing and reassuring to my personal and spiritual walk with God. So please put *23 Minutes in Hell* on your reading list. Of course, make sure you finish this one, first. Find out who you are in Christ before you dive into all of that. Don't allow the enemy to get you off course before you are ready for the next step in your divine journey. The leading truth is found primarily in the Word of God.

Spend time talking to God and reading His Word daily to be well fed by the Vine and growing in all the fruits of the Spirit. You will discover that the Holy Spirit will show you so many great things. He doesn't want you to be confused, afraid, or separated from Him. He is the best parent anyone could ever want or need. God is a good Papa, and He sent Jesus for you to be in a right relationship with the Father by whom you are adopted and engrafted into His family through His Son!

Big hugs,
Papa God and Ashley

The God Kind of Love

What is love? It has different meanings depending on what we are talking about or how we might feel about something. I love my husband and kids, but I can also say I love my car. Yet, I don't love my car the way I love my family. Scripture tells us what love is by God's definition: "Love is patient, love is kind. It does not envy, it does not boast, it is not proud. It does not dishonor others, it is not self-seeking, it is not easily angered, it keeps no records of wrongs. Love does not delight in evil but rejoices with the truth. It always protects, always trusts, always hopes, always perseveres. Love *never* fails" (1 Cor. 13:4–8 emphasis added).

How many times do we think like this in a day? When someone wrongs us, do our thoughts directly go to these Scriptures, or do we become the things that love is not?

I battle with these things on a regular basis myself. Someone pulls in front of my car, and I want to tell them off. If someone talks about me behind my back and what is said is not true, I want to get mad and yell at them for spreading false information about me.

But what good would that do? Does it solve the problem? It might correct the situation or make us feel a little better for setting things straight. But if we hold on to bitterness and scream at that person by saying things that are not kind in return, then aren't we are stooping down to a level we know we shouldn't go to ourselves? I am not saying you let people walk all over you. But it is how we handle the situation in love that makes the difference. Yes, sometimes we must put our foot down to protect what God has given us and healthy boundaries are good to establish.

Satan's main goal is to divide us. This is especially true when it comes to our families, even more so if you or your family is in ministry. That is what the enemy tried to do to my family, but I thank God for praying family members who didn't settle for the lies of the enemy. Family division can impact generation after generation and our own walk with God. Satan is a wolf who tries to separate the flock. We must be mindful of this. Think about what the enemy's goals are. If a specific tactic works every time, then why change the attack strategy?

Einstein said, "The definition of insanity is doing the same thing over and over again and expecting different results." If we keep reacting the same way out of frustration and anger to get a different result, we must change the way we react to hurtful situations. I heard my dad say in a sermon once, "If you want to change your circumstances, change the way you think."

Jesus walked in love, but many times He was bold and strong with His words, yet kind and loving in His approach. His words *always* lined up with God's words.

Listen, I understand that it is not easy to always walk in love. If it were, we would all be perfect like Jesus. That is why it is important to read the Word of God. The Bible is our manual to live happy and healthy lives so that we can train our thoughts to line up with His love and mercy.

Learn to pick and choose your battles; not every battle is worth fighting. Sometimes, walking away and asking God how to handle it is more important than our own words. If it is something that needs to be addressed and you have prayed about it, then approach that person or situation with wisdom. Sometimes the best thing to do in a heated moment is to say nothing. My brother Justin gave me some great wisdom I will never forget. He said, "Satan pushes, and God leads." God's ways are not stressful or pushy. His ways are calm and relaxed. We can defend ourselves in a way that is gentle while knowing that the truth wins the hearts and minds of others.

My youngest brother, Jordan, explained it like this: "Disagreements are misunderstandings. Each person believes they are in the right and the other is in the wrong."

Isn't the goal of expressing a point of view to help the other person understand where we are coming from and why there is disagreement? Taking a step back, thinking about the situation from the other person's perspective, and walking in love is the only way to come to a mature conclusion.

Here is something to ponder that might surprise some to hear: Jesus wasn't a popular guy to many people who disagreed with Him. Why do you think they crucified Him? They hated what He stood for. They did not understand, or maybe they didn't care that He was who He said He was. They wanted their way because they loved their sin. That basic concept hasn't changed even today. I love what Jesus said on the cross about His beloved children. "Jesus said, 'Father, forgive them, for they do not know what they are doing'" (Luke 23:34).

While He hung on the cross, Jesus forgave those people and their future generations. How can we justify crucifying someone else with our words when Jesus already forgave us and them? Who are we that we can make this judgment? It's not up to us to teach someone a lesson or even to make them understand our point of view. But it is up to us to let God teach us and transform our hearts to love others and forgive them the way God loves and forgives us.

Forgiveness doesn't mean you forget what was said or what happened. It means you give it to God and keep moving along the path set before you. Know this: God is love. If Jesus is your Lord, then His love is already in you. We should be practicing these things daily. The more you practice and seek God, the better you will get at walking in His love.

> Dear friend, let us love one another for love comes from God. Everyone who loves has been born of God and knows God. Whoever does not love does not know God, because God is love. This is how God showed his love among us: He sent his one and only Son into the world that we might live through Him. This is love: not that we loved God, but that He loved us and sent His Son as an atoning sacrifice for our sins. Dear friends, since God so loved us, we also ought to love one another. No one has ever seen God; but if we love one another, God lives in us and His love is made complete in us. (1 John 4:7–12)

You never know what someone is going through or has to deal with in their life. Maybe they have never had the opportunity to be loved by someone who truly cares for them. The love of God is foreign to them, and, therefore, God's love is not in them, but God still loves them.

If that person is truly unapproachable and hurtful, love them from a distance. I have learned that if I can't be around a person, there is still something I am called to do for them. God expects us to pray for those who persecute us. Praying with a whole heart and good intentions is a way to love them the same way God loves them. Then let God do what only He can do best. Find Scriptures that pertain to the love of God and pray those Scriptures over that person or people. One of my favorite Scriptures is from Ezekiel. I have prayed this verse over others and even over myself from time to time. "I will give you a new heart and put a new spirit in you; I will remove from you your heart of stone and give you a heart of flesh" (Ezek. 36:26)

As Christians, sometimes we are the only Jesus people see. If we have a heart of stone, we're not acting like Christ. I encourage you to get Scriptures of God's love so deeply rooted in your heart that nothing the enemy can do will stop you from showing Jesus to all who need to know His love through you.

If God is love, His love is already in us. Jesus died and rose again to reconcile us to the Father, and He released us from the prison of sin and death. The Holy Spirit showed me that Jesus is the key to free us from the jail of unforgiveness because of His love. As ambassadors of Christ, we already hold the key to love and forgiveness because Jesus loves and forgives us. Holding onto unforgiveness is pride and self-centeredness. Let us look at God's says about forgiveness.

> Therefore, as God's chosen people, holy and dearly loved, clothe yourselves with compassion, kindness, humility, gentleness and patience. Bear with each other and forgive one another if any has a grievance against someone. Forgive as the Lord forgave you. And over all these virtues put on love, which binds them all together in perfect unity. (Col. 3:12–14)

When we choose to hold anger toward another, it is basically saying, I don't care what Jesus did even though I have sinned against God and man. This is setting us above God with the mindset that our way is better than His way. Forgiveness is laying down our pride at the cross and allowing Jesus to take on that burden with His strength and God's love. Love is a commandment, not an option. "My command is this: Love each other as I have loved you. Greater love has no one than this: to lay down one's life for one's friends. You are my friends if you do what I command" (John 15:12–14).

God knows that it is a challenge to forgive someone who has wronged you. The more time you spend with someone, the more you become like them, don't you? So the more time you spend with God in fellowship, the more you learn about His ways, and that His ways are good. Forgiving someone in our own efforts can be almost impossible, but with the help of the Holy Spirit, all things are possible because He is our helper.

Knowing this truth, isn't it time to set ourselves and the other person(s) free from the prison of unforgiveness? Jesus did because He loves us, and God is the real meaning and purpose of love.

Big hugs,
Papa God and Ashley

The Persistent Widow

During the week, I wake up early before the rest of the family to sit in my office or family room and spend time with the Papa God. It's my quiet time with Him. Like most people, sometimes my flesh wants to go back to bed and sleep for that extra hour. One day, I had been facing some big decisions, and I thought as I slowly walked to my office, "Papa God, is this doing me any good to get up and do this so early? I am so tired, and my body and mind feel so weary."

But like a good little duck that follows the leading of the Holy Spirit, I sat down and put my Bible on my lap and prayed, "Lord, lead me in Your Word and to what You want me to know. I need to hear You today. I don't want to just sit here and read to learn. I need to know what You have to say about my situation or what's on Your heart and mind for me today."

It is so amazing how He will speak to us with exactly what we are feeling or thinking through His written Word. That morning, He took me to Luke 18 about the persistent widow and the unjust judge.

On that particular day, I had been feeling that all I did was pray, pray, pray for so many things and so many people. I said to Papa God,

"I do see the fruit of my labor in many ways, but there are those things in life that seem to take so long!" I found myself saying to God, "Come on, Lord! What is the hold-up here? I have been fasting, praying, and calling on You, Lord, in my times of trouble and need. What more can I do, Lord?"

You see, God is a just and faithful God. Sometimes we pray for things with the right heart and intentions, but we want things to happen in our timing. Here's what we tend to forget in those waiting moments: God knows the beginning to the end, and His timing is perfect. If your prayers line up with the will of the Father (written in your Bible) like health, healing, family, finances, and work issues, there is nothing wrong with us asking and praying for those requests we bring to God. If God had a problem with it, He would have taken the story of the persistent widow altogether out of the Bible. "And the Lord said, 'Listen to what the unjust judge says. And will not God bring about justice for His chosen ones, who cry out to him day and night? Will He keep putting them off? I tell you, He will see that they get justice, and quickly. However, when the Son of Man comes, will he find faith on earth?'" (Luke 18:6–8).

God knows our hearts. It is for His glory that will shine in the darkest hours for all to see what He has accomplished through those trials and troubles. Just when you think of giving up, don't. Keep going! God will never leave you or forsake you. His Word is true, and He is always with you.

Persistence is not nagging God or trying to make Him do something for us. It is the persistence of faith and believing God has (fill in the blank with the issue) in the palms of His hands. It is being diligent, even when we don't see the results we need right away. All too often, people want to try and force God to do what they want Him to do. They will never reap the rewards of what God will do for them with this approach.

God loves us. He is not withholding anything from us to be difficult. Often, I believe there are things happening behind the scenes that we just don't see with our natural eyes. It is our job as Christians to keep praying and expecting God to work on our behalf. God said to come boldly to His throne of grace and make your request to Him.

To answer my own question of is it worth it to get up early and spend time with Papa God, the answer is a big *yes*! I have learned so much in those quiet times with God. It is in those times that answers come and breakthroughs emerge.

> For the LORD gives wisdom; from his mouth comes knowledge and understanding. He holds success in store for the upright, he is a shield to those whose walk is blameless, for He guards the course of the just and protects the way of his faithful ones. Then you will understand what is right and just and fair—every good path. (Prov. 2:6–9)

Thank God for His wisdom today. Keep being persistent; keep asking and believing that God will come through for you. Quality time with Papa God is worth it! If you keep seeking Him and His wisdom, the Holy Spirit will speak His ways and guide you into His truth to healing and wholeness. Once you hear the answer, be obedient to His direction, and you will walk through the doors He has planned for you.

Big hugs,
Papa God and Ashley

Test the Spirits

When fear and doubt enter in your mind, have you ever wondered if God was talking to you, or if it was the enemy talking? I know I have.

Basically, we hear three voices in our thoughts: the soul (God's voice), our own thoughts, and the enemy's. I have learned that not every thought that comes into my head is my own. And just because I think it, does not mean it is true.

It is not true until we put that thought into action. Once we act on the thought, that makes it true, and the thought becomes our own. This is what the Word says about casting down those thoughts. "We demolish arguments and every pretension that sets itself up against the knowledge of God, and we take captive every thought to make it obedient to Christ. And we will be ready to punish every act of disobedience, once your obedience is complete" (2 Cor. 10:5–6).

We realize by this Scripture that we have a choice. We can either listen to the wrong ideas or take authority over them and tell them to go in the name of Jesus. Obedience to the Word of God is saying what God says about the situation.

In Sherry Grace Anderson's book, *Prophetic Boot Camp Basic Training for the 21st Century*, she tells a story about when her kids were finally old enough to be left at home alone for a short time so she could go to the grocery store and do some shopping. I recall Sherry telling this story because it woke me up to how the enemy works with his lies and deceit. She wrote that a thought had entered her head saying, "Something is wrong at home; you better get back now!" It seemed so urgent that she thought, "Oh my gosh, something is going on, and the kids need me." All of a sudden she recalled 1 John 4:1–3. This is what it says:

> Dear friends, do not believe every spirit but test the spirits to see whether they are from God because many false prophets have gone out into the world. This is how you can recognize the Spirit of God: Every spirit that acknowledges that Jesus Christ has come in the flesh is from God, but every spirit that does not acknowledge Jesus is not from God. This is the spirit of the antichrist, which you have heard is coming and even now is already in the world. (1 John 4:1–3)

So she said these words, "Does the spirit that is talking confess Jesus Christ has come in the flesh?" To her surprise, there was no answer. Confident the Holy Spirit had prompted her that her kids were safe, she finished her shopping and then went home. When she got there, she was right on. Nothing was wrong, and everyone was OK.

I am so glad I read that story and felt led to share it with you. You see, Satan and his demons cannot confess Jesus is God in the flesh, that Jesus is the Lord incarnated in a human body. This is because they are liars, and they hate the blood of Jesus. They can't stand against it and try their best to mess with us and make us afraid. The name of Jesus is the most powerful weapon against the enemy. Demons tremble at His name and Jesus gave us His name to use against the enemy.

Therefore, God exalted him to the highest place and gave him the name that is above every name, that at the name of Jesus every knee should bow, in heaven and on earth and under the earth, and every tongue acknowledge that Jesus Christ is Lord, to the glory of God the Father. Therefore, my dear friends, as you have always obeyed—not only in my presence, but now much more in my absence—continue to work out your salvation with fear and trembling, for it is God who works in you to will and to act in order to fulfill his good purpose. (Phil. 2:9–13)

Everything is subject to the name of Jesus, and every knee must bow to that name. The enemy is held hostage from lying to you when you use the name above all names. It doesn't mean he won't try again, but when this happens, strike the enemy back again with the name of Jesus. Whenever you find yourself in a situation where a thought like this comes to your mind and you don't know what to do, step aside somewhere quiet and verbally ask that question Sherry asked. If you get no answer, you know who's talking! Then go along about your business.

I hope this ah-ha moment has set you free from this tactic of the enemy. I have used it many times, and guess what? I knew who was talking!

The more time you spend with Papa God and you learn what your legal rights are in the Spirit, the easier it will become to distinguish the thoughts and the voices speaking to you. It is imperative to note that all our words must line up with the Word of God. If they don't, they are false. I'm not saying that the Holy Spirit can't warn you of incoming danger or to be on guard. What I am saying is to confirm from where the source is coming.

Big hugs,
Papa God and Ashley

Wrongly Accused

Have you ever been accused of something you did not do? To be wrongly accused is a tough pill to swallow, and hurt feelings seem to follow the unjust accusation. In a just world, I think we would all agree that the person who actually did the dishonorable deed needs to stand up and take responsibility for their actions. That is why we have trials with a judge, defense, offense, and a group of outsiders also known as the jury who can hear the story and make a logical judgment call without bias.

Considering the way our legal system is set up, I think about the kingdom of God and how our earthly life mirrors this system. Because we live in a fallen world, I often feel that God is wrongly accused. I constantly hear statements like, "God, why did You let this person die?" or "Why did You allow me to get sick?" or "God why did You _____ (fill in the blank)?"

I can play the role of the defense attorney; let me take you (the jury) back to the real culprit and the sin of "The accuser of our souls." Let's go back to the Garden of Eden when God made Adam and Eve in the book of Genesis. When "mankind" (male and female) were created,

God made them in His image. He gave them authority to rule over the earth and all that inhabited it.

> Then God said, "Let us make mankind in our image, in our likeness, so that they may rule over the fish in the sea and the birds in the sky, over the livestock and all the wild animals, and over all the creatures that move along the ground." So, God created mankind in his own image, in the image of God he created them; male and female he created them. God blessed them and said to them, "Be fruitful and increase in number; fill the earth and subdue it. Rule over the fish in the sea and the birds in the sky and over every living creature that moves on the ground." (Gen. 1:26–28)

After the creation of Adam and Eve, that sneaky snake, Satan, came and slithered his way into the garden to deceive them.

> Now the snake was the most cunning animal that the LORD God had made. The snake asked the woman, "Did God really tell you not to eat fruit from any tree in the garden?" "We may eat the fruit of any tree in the garden," the woman answered, "except the tree in the middle of it. God told us not to eat the fruit of that tree or even touch it; if we do, we will die." The snake replied, "That's not true; you will not die. God said that because he knows that when you eat it, you will be like God and know what is good and what is bad." The woman saw how beautiful the tree was and how good its fruit would be to eat, and she thought how wonderful it would be to become wise. So she took some of the fruit and ate it. Then she gave some to her husband, and he also ate it. As soon as they had eaten it, they were given understanding and realized that they were naked; so, they sewed fig leaves together and covered themselves. That evening they heard the LORD God walking in the garden, and they hid from him among the trees. But the LORD God called out to the man, "Where are you?" (Gen. 3:1–9 GNT)

I find that last statement from God intriguing. He said to Adam and Eve, "Where are you?" Now let's not even begin to pretend that God did not know where they were physically. What He was really asking them was, "Where are you spiritually?" I believe that He was saying, "Something has happened, and I feel a separation from you. Why have you fallen away from Me?"

In the garden, God had a close relationship with Adam and Eve. They were very smart; after all, they were given full reign and authority to name all the animals, plants, and things on this earth. Contrary to what this world wants to tell you, Adam was not a caveman. I repeat, Adam was not a caveman! He was not trying to rub two sticks together to figure out how to make fire and live. Adam had the favor of God on him and the breath of almighty God in him. (See Gen. 2:7.) Let's think about that for a second. The very breath of God who also breathes out the stars when He speaks was in Adam. If God is beyond our intelligence then Adam had to be intelligent, too. (See Ps. 33:6.)

When Adam sinned against God, he knew what happened, and that he committed high treason against God and himself. He told Eve that God had said, "To not to eat that forbidden fruit." She was deceived by Satan, but she did it anyway because she wanted to, and so did Adam. The problem is, like most people who sin, they know it is wrong. They even know there will be a consequence for the action, but it looks good, it may even smell good, and so it must be OK to be consumed. That's why when someone does something they know is wrong, they lie to try and avoid the consequence. The forbidden fruit or bait is the sin.

One day, out of my own frustration, I said to God, "Lord if Eve is in heaven, I am going to march right up to her and tell her off for making me go through female pain every month and during childbirth."

God answered me right back and said, "How many apples have you bitten in your life, Ashley?"

I thought, "Ouch! God, that hurt." I call those remarks from God spiritual spankings. And you know what? God is right; it is so true. When God asked Adam about the sin of eating the forbidden fruit, he immediately pointed his finger at Eve and God. "The man said, 'The woman you put here with me—she gave me some fruit from the tree, and I ate it.' Then the LORD God said to the woman, 'What is this you have done?' The woman said, 'The serpent deceived me, and I ate" (Gen. 3:12–13).

They both wanted to blame someone other than themselves, even though they both knew they were wrong. The Bible doesn't tell us what Satan said. For all we know, after God told off the snake, he probably just grinned and slithered away like the snake he is. Satan knew what he was doing when he deceived both Adam and Eve. He wanted the authority God had given them, and he got it. Satan stripped Adam and Eve of their dominion.

This tactic of Satan is still being played out even today. Satan still tries to deceive God's children into thinking that he is bigger than God, and that he still has the authority over us. This is a lie. Satan only has authority or control in our lives if we give it to him. Jesus now has authority over Satan because He defeated him, and if Jesus is living in you, He has given that authority (His name) for you to use.

My point is that we can point fingers at others and God all day long, but the reality is we all sin, and we all need a Savior—Jesus Christ. Every one of us has listened to the enemy's lies and bitten the forbidden fruit of sin at some point. Thank you, Jesus, that God already had a plan of redemption even before the foundation of the earth, before Adam and Eve sinned. "For if, by the trespass of the one man, death reigned through that one man, how much more will those who receive God's abundant provision of grace and of the gift of righteousness reign in life through the one man, Jesus Christ!" (Rom. 5:17).

To sum this Scripture up in easy terms, "one man, death reigned" is Adam. The "gift of righteousness (right standing) through One man to reign in life" is Jesus. Do you see that?

Here is a very important part of this story. I want you to get this. God is not to blame when we sin, when we are sick, or even if someone dies before their time. God is a merciful God who has great compassion and love for His children. "The thief comes only to steal and kill and destroy; I have come that they may have life, and have it to the full" (John 10:10).

Satan is the liar, murderer, and deceiver, but redemption was paid in full for our sin with the royal blood of Jesus Christ on the cross at Calvary.

God had a message for that sneaky snake right before he slithered away. We will find it in Genesis when God foretold His plan of redemption. He explained how He would use a woman to give birth to the Messiah who would come to crush Satan's head. This is so exciting! "And I will put enmity between you and the woman, and between your offspring and hers; he will crush your head, and you will strike his heel" (Gen. 3:15).

It's not who you are or where you're from, and it's not what you have or haven't done. It's not how good or bad you've been. When Adam sinned, we all fell with him. But Jesus was the second Adam, and He got it right! I'll say it again boldly: *Jesus bought us back with His blood on Calvary, not counting our sins against us because of the fall of the one man, Adam. Hallelujah!*

All this is from God, who reconciled us to himself through Christ and gave us the ministry of reconciliation: that God was reconciling the world to himself in Christ, not counting people's sins against them. And he has committed to us the message of reconciliation. We are therefore Christ's ambassadors, as though God were making his appeal through us. We implore you on Christ's behalf: Be reconciled to God. (2 Cor. 5:18–20)

Isn't that great news? What God wants from us in return is our love and faith in the One who came to make all things new. Jesus came to set things straight, back to the original intention for Papa God's children; God wants a family. God had a plan all the way back in the beginning to legally claim us back as His own. Jesus accomplished this because He is God in the flesh, and His blood is what bought us back from the slavery of sin and death. God had to have a human body with royal blood to override what Adam did.

Just like Adam and Eve had a choice, we all have a choice to follow the Word of God or listen to the enemy. Yes, because of Adam and Eve's sin we all must live in a fallen world. Satan is the true culprit and the one to blame. Before God cast Satan out of heaven, he was trying to overthrow God. He wanted, and still wants, to be God, but he can't.

Consider that statement. I can't be someone I am not. You can't be me, and I can't be you. Jealousy is an awful cancer that hardens hearts and brings hatred to all who get in the path of the one in sin, so it makes total sense that Satan would try to deceive God's most precious possession, His beloved mankind.

God made you in His image. He loves you so much that He would send His only Son to die in your place for something He did not do. Now that is love, and that is one awesome God.

If you have blamed God for something or someone who has wronged you, God wants you to make it right.

My assignment to write this is to teach others how to have a relationship with Him and what our rightful place is as Christians in this fallen world. People get so caught up in religion and in pointing the finger at others they forget that all God wants is a relationship with us. They forget that Jesus paid the consequence for what Adam did.

Don't take the same bait Satan has used from the beginning. I'll tell you a secret. When things continue to go wrong in my life and I am done playing games with Satan, I remind him that he lost this battle over two thousand years ago. Jesus was and is that enmity who God told Satan about before he slithered his ugly, stinky tail out of the garden (see Gen. 3:15).

I tell him, "Satan you can slither your high stinky tail on out of here! My Papa God is bigger than you. He's better than you, and Jesus lives in me. Because of the blood of Jesus, I now have the authority to tell you to stop your tricks and get lost, in the name of Jesus." I encourage you to get bold with Satan, too.

This is the best part: Satan and his minions must listen and bow to the name of Jesus because they know the price paid, and that redemption was made on the cross. Satan may be the culprit for all the destruction since the fall of Adam, but Jesus is the One with the victory! Everything that Jesus gained back for us also belongs to you and me. The word *Christian* means "Christ-Ins" meaning we are *in Christ Jesus.* There are several Scriptures on what belongs to believers who are in Christ. Look them up and find out what belongs to you *in* Christ. There is a great little book by Kenneth E. Hagin that you should purchase called *In Him.* It's one of those books that I carry with me, and I like to hand them out to people because it's a very small but powerful book to study regarding what rightfully belongs to Christians.

Until you're able to get your hands on this book, I'm giving you some homework. Look up these Scriptures and underline them in your Bible. If you learn who you are in Christ, you will be unstoppable in the kingdom of God. Kenneth E. Hagin lists these Scriptures about being in Christ in his book.

Romans 3:24	Galatians 2:4	Philippians 3:13–14
Romans 8:1–2	Galatians 3:26	Colossians 1:28
Romans 12:5	Galatians 3:28	1 Thessalonians 4:16
1 Corinthians 1:2	Galatians 5:6	1 Thessalonians 5:18

1 Corinthians 1:30	Galatians 6:14	1 Timothy 1:14
1 Corinthians 15:22	Ephesians 1:3	2 Timothy 1:9
2 Corinthians 1:21	Ephesians 1:10	2 Timothy 2:1
2 Corinthians 2:14	Ephesians 2:6	2 Timothy 3:15
2 Corinthians 3:14	Ephesians 2:10	Philemon 1:6
2 Corinthians 5:17	Ephesians 2:13	1 Peter 1:8
2 Corinthians 5:19	Ephesians 3:6	1 John 2:5-9

You can also look up Scriptures on the following topics:

in Him	by Himself	with Christ
in whom	by His blood	with Him
in the Lord	by whom	by Me
by Him	from whom	in Me
by Christ	through Christ	in My love
in the beloved	through Him	in His name

Most Bibles have a concordance in the back to look up keywords and Scriptures. I like computers, and the fastest way I have looked up these Scriptures is to word search them on the Internet and then look up the Scriptures on Biblegateway.com. There are other sources, but this is the method I like to use.

I use colored pencils and change the color for each category. For example, I underline the Scriptures on "in Him" in blue and the Scriptures on "in Christ" in purple. Then in the same color pencil, I write those Scriptures in the front of my Bible. This way it was easy for me to find them when I flip to the chapter and verse. Once I find the Scripture, I speak them out loud to myself or to someone else.

You can use other Scriptures using this method and make declarations over yourself and others. Here is an example to help you understand what I am saying. Let's use the verse, John 3:16. I will place my name in the Scripture so that I am personally a part of this verse. "For God so loved Ashley, that He gave His only begotten Son, that if Ashley believes in Him, she will not perish, but will have everlasting life."

Many Scriptures are prayers. The apostle Paul wrote letters to the Ephesians from his heart as if they were prayers for them. These prayers were written so that readers could learn to walk in the victory of the Word of God as His chosen people and royal priesthood. "But you are a chosen people, a royal priesthood, a holy nation, God's special possession, that you may declare the praises of him who called you out of darkness into his wonderful light" (1 Peter 2:9).

Truly, the more we speak words over ourselves or others, the more these attributes start to become part of that person's character. As we learn who we are in Christ and what we have as King's kids, our way of thinking will shift to God's way of thinking. This is because our confidence grows stronger and stronger when we believe what we are saying. Soon others will take notice of the changes, too. This goes back to the butterfly changes we spoke of earlier. The more you read your Bible and say what God says, the faster the metamorphosis of spiritual growth occurs. Again, this is what the Bible means when it says we renew our minds. We go back to Scripture over and over until we get it and act on it. I purposefully gave you the Scripture 1 Peter 2:9 so that you would know who God says you are. As a believer in Christ, you are a child of the King of all kings.

I want you to imagine yourself as a prince or a princess and your father is the king of England. You live in the most beautiful castle in the land, and your father is the ruler. Everyone and everything is subject to your command, but one day you wake up and think, "I don't feel like royalty today." You get out of bed and go down to the kitchen and take off your royal clothes and crown and start cleaning the floors and the dishes instead of someone serving your breakfast. Due to your mindset, you start acting like a servant instead of a prince or princess. Now imagine that the staff members in the castle notice your behavior. They would think you were out of your mind and start talking about you. They might say things like, "What's going on? Did someone forget they are royalty today?"

Well, maybe you do clean the floors and clean the dishes in your own home. That's OK. I clean my floors and do the dishes in my home, too. My point is this: God is higher than any earthly king. As a child of the most high God, we must know who we are. People will treat you differently when you know who you are. Truthfully, you will treat yourself differently when you discover what God says about you.

If you struggle with this confidence, I would like to suggest that you take the time to write thirty-one Scriptures on the topics of *in Christ, in Him,* and *in whom* on note cards and set one aside to read each day. You can also do this on your smartphone or computer. The point is to get who you are in Christ so deeply rooted in your thoughts that nothing or no one can tell you otherwise. Start declaring these Scriptures over yourself. Let's try this with Romans 8:1–2. The full Scripture is given below and then I revised it to relate to you specifically.

Therefore, there is now no condemnation for those who are in Christ Jesus, because through Christ Jesus the law of the Spirit who gives life has set you free from the law of sin and death. (Rom. 8:1–2)

Now I would say this Scripture about myself like this:

Therefore, there is now no condemnation for *me* because I am in Christ Jesus, because through Christ Jesus the law of the Spirit who gives *me* life and has set *me* free from the law of sin and death.

Oh, my gosh! Isn't that an amazing promise from God to you? When the enemy comes and whispers lies about your past in your ears, say this Scripture and others like it to yourself. If someone brings up what you did before your salvation, you simply say, "That's not what my God says about me. Romans 8:1–2 says I am set free from condemnation because I am in Christ Jesus. The Spirit of God set me free from that old way of life, and I am a new creation in Christ. There is no one else like me. I know who I belong to, and my God loves me. Jesus paid the price for my sins, and I am no longer a part of that old pattern of life and death."

I pray this helps you to know who you are in Christ and who the real culprit is. Satan is a liar, and he can't come around to steal what rightfully belongs to you as a Christ follower if you know who you are. No longer can you be wrongly accused because Jesus already paid the penalty for your life.

So get fired up. Your life is about to change rapidly if you get these Scriptures deeply rooted in your soul!

Big hugs,
Papa God and Ashley

The World Champion

One night, about 2 o'clock in the morning, Papa God woke me up and started telling me this story about Mr. Virtuous and Mr. Ruthless. God gave me this vision right before I went through one of my most challenging times. I did not realize at the time of the vision that this story would play out before my eyes in the weeks and years to come. I had many difficult decisions to make, both in the natural and the spiritual worlds. There were times that I fell into a great depression because of the circumstances and decisions from others that greatly impacted my life. Looking back, I see that the outcome of this story would be that I had to be fully surrendered to God's will and purpose for my life. My character was being challenged, and I had to walk by faith like never before. The good news is that He never left my side through it all.

As you read this story, I want you to use your full imagination and envision the characters. This vision played out like a movie for me, and Papa God would not allow me to rest until I wrote it down, word for word.

There were many times during this challenging time that I would go back and read this story to give me the strength and courage I needed to keep moving ahead. Only Papa God knew I would need this story to get through that time in my life.

Imagine watching a boxing match. When the boxers first come out on stage they are all pumped up and jumping up and down. They might even roll their heads around, stretching out their necks, pumping their arms back and forth in a good stretch. Both fighters look totally muscular and fit, ready and willing to fight their opponent.

Imagine their boxing shorts and gloves. One opponent, Virtuous Guy, is wearing white, while the other opponent, Ruthless Guy, is wearing black.

The ruthless opponent might even mock both the crowd and the virtuous opponent. He looks tough and cruel as he paces back and forth in a slow, methodical motion. He even has some scary scars on his face because he has done so much fighting and bullying.

The announcer comes on the loudspeakers announcing the names of the contestants: "In the left corner is Mr. Ruthless, the Liar!" Suddenly, beams of light in the arena start moving faster and faster, and the music is loud and sinister. Mr. Ruthless starts playing out his display of rude behavior with his fist moving in a fast boxing like motion toward the other contestant.

The crowd goes wild in boos and hisses! There may be some in the crowd who are rooting for the guy in black, but there is only a handful who display their affection. Yet, they are still loud and definitely noticed.

A few seconds later, the mood changes, and the music starts an anthem-like song. The room goes dark and the spotlight shines brightly on the virtuous opponent, and all eyes are on him. The announcer comes on the loud speaker again and says, "And in the right corner is Mr. Virtuous, the Man of Truth!" The crowd of onlookers goes crazy screaming and jumping up and down, rooting for their hoped-for champion.

The referee in a black and white striped shirt suddenly enters the ring and asks the two opponents to come together and do a quick handshake. Mr. Ruthless tries to avoid the nice gestures but knows the rules and does a hard fist bump to Mr. Virtuous.

Then the bell rings: "Ding, ding!" The referee quickly moves out of the way, ready to judge the fight.

The fight is on! Mr. Ruthless moves in quick for the attack on Mr. Virtuous and knocks him back. You can see the stunned look in Mr. Virtuous's eyes, but he comes back with his fists up and ready for the next punch. He swings as hard as he can and knocks Mr. Ruthless back. Mr. Ruthless then comes back harder. This happens a few more times. Over and over, the blows come. Then Mr. Ruthless packs a powerful punch, giving Mr. Virtuous a black eye and knocking him to the ground.

The fight is intense, but Mr. Virtuous is not finished, and he gets back up! But the bell barely rings again, and before he knows it, Mr. Ruthless comes out of nowhere and knocks him down again.

Now he is badly hurt. The bell rings again, and Mr. Virtuous gets back up, ready this time for another sucker punch because he has learned that Mr. Ruthless is a sneaky cheater. Feeling suddenly dizzy and faint, Mr. Virtuous requests a short time out, which is granted by the referee.

Mr. Virtuous barely makes it over to his coach (who is dressed in white, by the way). They say a quick prayer and take a drink of water. Then Mr. Virtuous is back in the ring and ready for the fight. He has a renewed strength that he didn't quite have before. The look in his eyes is determined, and he looks Mr. Ruthless dead on. His gaze is laser focused on and toward Mr. Ruthless. Mr. Virtuous is serious, and Mr. Ruthless feels a shudder up his spine. Mr. Virtuous has never been readier than right this moment for this fight.

Mr. Ruthless is nervous, and he makes the first swing and misses. Then he comes back again with a left hook and yet misses Mr. Virtuous again! Mr. Virtuous seems to be moving with ease, side to side with each left and right swing coming at him. Suddenly, Mr. Virtuous realizes what he needs to do to knock out his opponent. He cries out in a loud yell, "*Jesus!*" And he throws his right fist so hard that in just one swing, Mr. Ruthless goes down hard to the ground.

The crowd gives out a big gasp in unison. The referee jumps up and runs over to Mr. Ruthless to check if he is still coherent. The crowd looks on, intently waiting for the results. To everyone's surprise, Mr. Ruthless is out cold. The referee takes Mr. Virtuous by the arm and holds his hand up in the air as the champion. The crowd goes wild!

Have you ever felt like you were in the fight of your life? The enemy looks like he is coming after you, and he is very intimidating. At first, you are confident. You know who is in your corner, but with every passing second, the enemy is coming at you so hard you feel like giving up. That is when you take a break and spend time with God. He fills you up with everything you need, and you are then ready to take down your ruthless opponent. But you can't do it without the Word of God. The water is the refreshing you need because it is the water of life, and the prayer is your connecting with God. Then you are filled up with the Holy Spirit and ready for the fight.

We all love a happy ending when Virtuous Guy wins. But let's imagine that the story did not end that way. Imagine that Mr. Ruthless wins the fight. How disappointing is that? Mr. Virtuous goes down after the sucker punch, is too tired to get back up, and he looks over at the Man in White standing in the corner but just doesn't have any more fight left in him. He sits down and cries. He says to the Man in White, "I wish I could do this, but I am done." The crowd feels disappointment, and Mr. Virtuous feels shame and regret. Feeling pleasure in the defeat,

Mr. Ruthless mocks Mr. Virtuous and leaves him sitting there all alone. The lights go dark and everyone leaves the show disappointed.

What? "No! It can't end this way," you might say. But my friend, this happens every day to God's people who have the title of Mr. Virtuous because God created them to be a champion, but they don't know who they are in the kingdom of God and who lives inside of them.

They don't go to the Man in White in the corner, say a prayer, and take a drink of water, which is the fountain of life. They just give up because it seems too hard. They let the enemy walk away as the victor. God is in their corner, but they just don't trust that He has what they need to win the fight of their life.

God loves me so much that He gave me this story to keep my eyes on Him and to trust Him in this fight that came against me. I want to share what I learned through all of this because there were moments when I felt like the enemy, Mr. Ruthless, was punching me and knocking me to the ground. Scripture tells us what we need to do when we are in a battle. We are to put on the full armor of God.

Finally, be strong in the Lord and in his mighty power. Put on the full armor of God, so that you can take your stand against the devil's schemes. For our struggle is not against flesh and blood, but against the rulers, against the authorities, against the powers of this dark world and against the spiritual forces of evil in the heavenly realms. Therefore, put on the full armor of God, so that when the day of evil comes, you may be able to stand your ground, and after you have done everything, to stand. Stand firm then, with the belt of truth buckled around your waist, with the breastplate of righteousness in place, and with your feet fitted with the readiness that comes from the gospel of peace. In addition to all this, take up the shield of faith, with which you can extinguish all the flaming arrows of the evil one. Take the helmet of salvation and the sword of the Spirit, which is the word of God. And pray in the Spirit on all occasions with all kinds of prayers and requests. With this in mind, be alert and always keep on praying for all the Lord's people. Pray also for me, that whenever I speak, words may be given me so that I will fearlessly make known the mystery of the gospel, for which I am an ambassador in chains. Pray that I may declare it fearlessly, as I should. (Eph. 6:10–20)

Dear friend, please pay close attention to this Scripture about whom we essentially fight against. So many Christians make the mistake of fighting the wrong enemy. "For our struggle is not against flesh and blood, but against the rulers, against the authorities, against the powers of this dark world and against the spiritual forces of evil in the heavenly realms" (Eph. 6:12).

Did you see that? Get this Scripture deeply rooted in you. *We are in a fight with the rulers of the air, not a person (flesh and blood) or sickness and disease.*

Jesus already died and rose again. He is not still hanging on the cross waiting to win the battle. He has already won! Praise God. Now it is up to us (children of God) to take up those boxing gloves and fight the good fight of faith with the help of the Holy Spirit and the Word of God. "You, dear children, are from God and have overcome them because the one who is in you is greater than the one who is in the world" (1 John 4:4).

Who is "them" in this verse? Based on this Scripture, it's the rulers, the authorities, the powers of this dark world, and the spiritual forces of evil in the heavenly realms that we will overcome.

Who is the greater One who lives inside of you? That is our Jesus! Yes, scream that from the rooftops once you get this! If you have accepted Jesus as your Lord and Savior, then Jesus already lives in you. Don't give up in the middle of the fight and let the enemy win. Keep pressing forward. Put on your armor of God and win this battle!

My friend, I learned so much through that terrible experience, but God used it as a testimony to tell you that Satan cannot win. The devil already lost his authority when Jesus died, rose again, and sat down at the right hand of the Father. Because of what Jesus did, Ephesians 2:6–7 says we are seated at the right hand of the Father in heavenly places.

Now, because Jesus lives in your heart, *you* have the legal authority to tell Satan to get behind you. Use the name above all names, Jesus. Then knock the adversary out cold once and for all. Remember who you are. You are chosen. "But you are a chosen people, a royal priesthood, a holy nation, God's special possession, that you may declare the praises of him who called you out of darkness into his wonderful light" (1 Peter 2:9).

Don't be left sitting in the dark. Get back up and put all your focus and attention on the real enemy, and be the virtuous champion that you are chosen and called to be through the blood of Jesus Christ.

Find other prayer warriors to pray with you. God once told me, "You know, Ashley, you don't have to fight this battle all by yourself." I then made friends with like-minded people. I got involved with a local church, and that led to other friends who created prayer pages on social media sites that I could connect with as well. In addition, most churches have Bible studies and connection groups.

When I felt like giving up, these friends became my cheering crowd and helped me pray. Believe me, I have some feisty friends who know who God is, and they know who they are in Christ! They lead me back to the Word of God, and it quickly reminds me of who I am. This encouragement refreshes me and gives me the strength to keep going. I am so thankful for these friends.

Know this: The things of this world will battle for your devotion, your time, and your love. God never said this life would come without hard times, but He did say that the battles we go through will be worth it in the end if we keep the faith and our eyes on Him. Scripture says in Matthew 24:12–13 that those who stand firm to the end will be saved. That means troubles will try to follow us and even knock us back throughout our lives on this earth. We must keep the faith until the end.

From the beginning to the end of this battle, things didn't always go the way I had hoped or planned. Actually, quite the opposite happened. It seemed like the other team had won the battle, but God had the plan all along. This is what I learned throughout it all. The battle is already won and *Jesus is the true world champion*. No matter what happens in the natural realm, what we can see with our eyes or what we are told by others, God operates in the supernatural realm, and what He says, goes. God is the final judge in the end. Knowing this freed me from any bitterness or resentment of what was done by this group of people. I am not the judge, and openly, I am glad about that. That is a big responsibility I am not willing to take on. If I try to take on that role, it is saying I know more than God.

Still, we all have a part to play in our story. We must be diligent in our faith without wavering and walk out the process. Through it all, I learned a lot about myself, and it drew me closer to God in a way I hadn't known Him before. For that, I am grateful.

If you are going through a challenging time, don't give up. You can do this! I hope this testimony encourages you to keep going. If you get knocked down, get back up and focus on the real enemy. Then imagine how the crowd goes wild when you throw that knockout punch with the name of Jesus. All of heaven and earth are cheering you on. Ding! Ding!

Big hugs,
Papa God and Ashley

Healing Belongs to You

Did you know that Jesus never ever turned anyone away from being healed who asked and believed? Even the daughter of the woman who was not a Jew was healed because she asked Jesus in persistence.

The Faith of a Canaanite Woman

Leaving that place, Jesus withdrew to the region of Tyre and Sidon. A Canaanite woman from that vicinity came to him, crying out, "Lord, Son of David, have mercy on me! My daughter is demon-possessed and suffering terribly." Jesus did not answer a word. So, his disciples came to him and urged him, "Send her away, for she keeps crying out after us." He answered, "I was sent only to the lost sheep of Israel." The woman came and knelt before him. "Lord, help me!" she said. He replied, "It is not right to take the children's bread and toss it to the dogs." "Yes, it is, Lord," she said. "Even the dogs eat the crumbs that fall from their master's table." Then Jesus said to her, "Woman, you have great faith! Your request is granted." And her daughter was healed at that moment. (Matt. 15:21–28)

I love how this Canaanite woman knew who Jesus was and what He could do for her daughter. She was persistent and showed Him how much she needed His mercy. I can imagine her following Jesus through huge crowds of people. When she finally got His attention, she knelt before Him and cried out for His help. I believe Jesus knew He would heal her daughter, but He also wanted to know if she believed He was willing and able. I think Jesus could feel her heart for her daughter. The desperation in her voice was real, and she had hope that He would answer her plea. Hope creates faith, and her faith is what moved Jesus to grant her daughter's healing.

Another important point is that He wasn't calling her a dog. He was, at that moment, there for the Jewish people, to fulfill the covenant God made with Abraham. However, He was asking her this question because she already knew the answer. She was not a dog or less important to God. And even if she was less than perfect, her prayers were worthy to be answered because God loved her. When she asked about the crumbs that fall from the master's table, she was saying, "Why not healing for my daughter?" In other words, "There is no reason You can't, Lord, because I know You can."

I also feel that she needed to stand up and take responsibility for her child and take actions for her own sins. There is nothing like a good momma who stands up for her child. She would walk to the ends of the earth and back to help her child. In her eyes, even the crumbs, extra miracles from Jesus, would be worth gathering to see her daughter be made whole again. He wanted to see if she believed she was worthy and how much she was willing to lay aside of her own sins to gain access into the blessings Jesus had for her and her daughter. It is apparent that she was ready to lay those sins at the feet of Jesus. It is even more apparent that Jesus was willing, and He was obviously impressed with her faith.

I also wonder if Jesus was testing His disciples to see if they understood His love for everyone. When the disciples told her to go away, I can imagine that they were shocked when Jesus answered her request. This went against everything their religious leaders had taught them, but Jesus was setting an example of a new way of thinking, right in front of them. I am impressed that God is strategic in everything He does.

Friend, no matter what you have done in your life, you are worthy to be healed, delivered, and set free from sickness and demonic oppression when you repent of your sins. Are you ready to lay everything down at the feet of Jesus to be healed physically, emotionally, and spiritually? The Lord knows your heart. Everything we do and say comes from the heart.

I did a little research on the Canaanites because I really wanted to know who and what the people of Canaan believed. Many of the Canaanites led the Jews to worship idols and were considered a deterrent to the Jews and the mission Jesus was to fulfill in His role for the Jewish people. The Israelites had battled with the Canaanites for centuries, but there are stories of Canaanites in the Bible who did a lot of good for the Jewish people. A good example is the battle of Jericho. (In your spare time look up the story of the prostitute and the scarlet cord in the book of Joshua.)

When the Canaanite mother approached the Rabbi, she knew who she was and the conflict between her people and the Israelites, but she would not take no for an answer from Jesus. She was a sinner, and she knew it. I think it is important to note that Jesus did not send her away because of her nationality but indeed had compassion and mercy on her.

Remember, this account and the countless other healings that Jesus performed, happened before He hung on the cross at Calvary. So if Jesus healed this lady's daughter when He walked this earth, is healing still viable today for Christ-believers and unbelievers alike? The answer is yes. I think this story proves that the blood of Jesus covers a multitude of sins for all mankind, even those who may not feel they are worth it and those who some feel don't deserve it.

Modern-day miracles are a testimony that God is still in the healing business for all. I have seen people who didn't believe that Jesus died for them, and they were healed when someone prayed for them. And don't you know they are believers now?

My dad was a hippie in the seventies when my grandmother Morgan dragged him to a crusade in Atlanta, Georgia. It was there that he saw a little deaf boy receive his healing. After seeing this firsthand, my dad said a prayer and said, "God, if You are real, heal me too!" That was the night he was healed (physically and spiritually), and he ran to the front altar and gave his life to the Lord.

Ironically, this may have come about because of my mom praying that same prayer for him. She said, "God, if You are real, save my family." As you read earlier, God did accomplish restoration (healing spiritually) of my family into a relationship with Christ.

As I have mentioned previously, my dad is a pastor with his doctorate in divinity and has been pastoring his church, Word of Life, in Apopka, Florida, for over twenty-five years. God is no respecter of persons; healing is for anyone who wants it and believes.

Then Peter began to speak: "I now realize how true it is that God does not show favoritism but accepts from every nation the one who fears him and does what is right. You know the message God sent to the people of Israel, announcing the good news of peace through Jesus Christ, who is Lord of all. You know what has happened throughout the province of Judea, beginning in Galilee after the baptism that John preached—how God anointed Jesus of Nazareth with the Holy Spirit and power, and how he went around doing good and healing all who were under the power of the devil, because God was with him. (Acts 10:34–38)

Jesus came to earth to show us who God is and how to be like Jesus. When He died and rose again, He gave all power all authority to His sons and daughters. However, many Christians still walk around with sickness and disease for years. In my observation, I think that they just accept the fact that they are ill, believe this must be God's will and say, "This is the way that it will always be."

The very words out of their mouths contradict what the Word of God says. One of the strategic tactics of the devil is to attack our minds before he attacks our bodies. (James 4:7, 1 Peter 5:8.) If he can get us to think we can't be healed, then we won't ever be. I have even heard Christians say, "Healing was for those in the Bible only." Well if that was the case then God is a liar, and we know that's not true. (See Heb. 13:8.)

Listen, I am just as guilty of this bad habit by praying for things and then contradicting my prayer shortly after. I understand how difficult it can be to quote Scripture over ourselves when we feel horrible. I have prayed for others, and they have felt better right away. And I have prayed for myself and remained ill, or it took some time before I started to feel better. I believe it comes down to faith and how much we will tolerate from the enemy. All sickness is an attack and a lie from Satan. He convinces us that it's easier to believe God could heal someone else and maybe it's just not working for us. The same goes for praying for the salvation of others like my mom and grandmother Morgan did for our family. Our words are powerful, and prayer does work. The battle is in our souls (minds) and how we are controlling our own thoughts and our tongues.

Warning sirens should be going off in our heads when these defeated thoughts come. God loves us and wants all His beloved healed for His purposes and plans. We can't fulfill our purpose in life if we are at home sick or in the hospital almost dead.

We each have different levels of faith based on our personal experiences and understanding of Scripture. So what does Scripture say we do if this is the case? First, we are to pray for each other. This is what the body of Christ is purposed to do, and prayer works when aligned with the Word of God. We are to lift each other up and help one another increase our faith to know that Jesus is still the healer and deliverer. That is why it is imperative that we surround ourselves with like-minded believers. I don't care if you're the strongest Christian you know, or you're just recently saved. We need to all pray for each other and for those who still need to know that God loves them and that He wants everyone to be saved and healed.

Second, we are to learn what our rightful authority is as sons and daughters of God in the earth. The biggest self-deceiver is naivete. There is no excuse for not knowing the Word of God especially is this modern day of technology and easy access to the Bible on the Web. In my experience, I have seen that most people spend hours on social media instead of spending that time with God and reading their Bibles. God has called us for more than this. Now that you're awake to God's truth, what else should you be doing with your time?

The great commission is the last conversation Jesus had with His disciples before He ascended into heaven. He gave them instructions, so to speak, of what their job would be going forward. It was not a suggestion; it was a command.

Commission can be defined as: an instruction, command, or role given to a person or group or a group of people entrusted by a government or other official with authority to do something.

The Great Commission
Later Jesus appeared to the Eleven as they were eating; he rebuked them for their lack of faith and their stubborn refusal to believe those who had seen him after he had risen. He said to them, "Go into all the world and preach the gospel to all creation. Whoever believes and is baptized will be saved, but whoever does not believe will be condemned. And these signs will accompany those who believe: In my name, they will drive out demons; they will speak in new tongues; they will pick up snakes with their hands; and when they drink deadly poison, it will not hurt them at all; they will place their hands on sick people, and they will get well." After the Lord Jesus had spoken to them, he was

taken up into heaven and he sat at the right hand of God. Then the disciples went out and preached everywhere, and the Lord worked with them and confirmed his word by the signs that accompanied it. (Mark 16:14–20)

Verse 18 says, "They will place their hands on sick people and they *will* get well." Then He ascended into heaven and sat down next to God. Healing is still accessible and available in this day and age because Jesus said it was. The Lord is not still hanging on the cross waiting to heal people; He is at the right hand of the Father waiting for His children to use the authority He gave us with His name. *We Christians must take authority with the name of Jesus and tell that sickness to go in Jesus' name.*

The third step is to speak *to* the sickness and say what Jesus said. Tell it to go in the name of Jesus. In Mark 11:23, Jesus said to speak to the mountain, and it will be cast into the sea. When you speak to the sickness, believe that it is gone. The mountain is the obstacle standing in your way to wholeness.

I think there is something to be learned from the Canaanite woman because she wouldn't take no for an answer from Jesus. She went to Him and took care of business. She wanted her daughter free right then and there.

Think about it like this. If a stinky and stray dog walked into your clean house and started urinating all over your clean floor and then proceeded to rub his stinky self all over your furniture, what would you do? Would you say in a soft, timid voice, "Oh, my! Poor stinky dog, please go away; you're not supposed to be in here"? Then would you say, "I want him gone, but I just can't do anything about it"?

Heck no! You would get a broom, shotgun, or call the law to get that nasty, filthy dog out of your house. You would take care of business, wouldn't you?

Well, your body is the temple of the Holy Spirit. Sickness, cancer, and disease are beneath you. As Christians—Christ in us—we are seated with Him far above anything that would try to come against us. Sickness is literally under our feet.

> I pray that the eyes of your heart may be enlightened in order that you may know the hope to which he has called you, the riches of his glorious inheritance in his holy people, and his incomparably great power for us who believe. That power is the same as the mighty strength he exerted when he raised Christ from the dead and seated him at his right hand in the heavenly realms, far above all rule and authority, power and dominion, and every name that is invoked, not only in the present age but also in the one to come. And God placed all things under his feet and appointed him to be head over everything for the church, which is his body, the fullness of him who fills everything in every way. (Eph. 1:18–23)

Friend, if you are sick or know someone who is sick, have great confidence knowing that Jesus already paid the price for our healing, and your faith is what moves God. Faith is to keep believing even when we don't see the results right away in the natural realm. This is a great time to find your way to the feet of Jesus and get down on your knees like the Canaanite woman and declare healing. I have learned two very important things about healing. The first is to speak healing Scriptures over myself or others who are sick. Our bodies are designed to respond to the written Word of God because there is life in the Word. (Say only what God says, anything in opposition to the truth is a contradiction to your prayers.) The enemy's attacks cannot stand against the Word of God and blood of Jesus. After reciting the Word, then plead the blood of Jesus over the body.

The second important factor in receiving your healing is to forgive others who have wronged you. Unforgiveness is a trap of the enemy to stop your healing and keep you from being set free from the deception of the enemy. Jesus was very specific about forgiving others. After all,

Jesus died for us even when we did not deserve His forgiveness and mercy. Read the parable of the unmerciful servant. (See Matt. 18:21–25.)

The great king in the parable, who is truly God, forgave a very large debt of the servant and in return, that servant did not have mercy on a smaller debt owed to him by a fellow servant. The punishment for the unmerciful servant was death.

I want to make known that I am not saying you should stay away from treatment by a doctor. I believe God gives wisdom to doctors to help us. However, when the situation goes beyond human ability, we need to seek the Word of God to live. There is an amazing book by Trina Hankins that I want to recommend to you. It's called, *God's Healing Word, A Practical Guide to Receiving Divine Healing.* There are so many wonderful testimonies about how God healed Trina and others in this book, and it is covered with healing Scriptures to repeat over yourself and/or your loved one.

The Lord is waiting to set you or your loved one free. He wants to know if you believe it and are obedient to His Word. If you are serious about your healing or the healing of someone else, get your Bible out, highlight all the Scriptures on healing, and start speaking them over yourself or your loved one. Our words change our circumstances. In the natural realm, it might seem like there is a battle going on, but Jesus already won the war. Know who you are and how precious you are to Papa God. I don't know your circumstances or where you come from, but it may be time for you to seek God with great persistence. Take your rightful seat of authority with Christ and just like the Canaanite woman, take care of business. God always causes us to triumph in victory! Then thank Him for what Jesus already did for you. There's work to do for the kingdom of God, and healing does belong to you.

Big hugs,
Papa God and Ashley

Facing Difficult Conversations

Sometimes it is hard for Christians to stand up in front of someone who is saying or acting the opposite of what we believe. Scripture tells us to be bold and stand against anything that is contrary to the Word of God. However, Scripture also says to walk in love always, so there should be a balance, right?

I had a conversation with someone recently that got me thinking about standing up in the face of adversity and speaking the truth in love. Depending on the situation when confronting someone who is deceived, it is important what is said and how it is said.

I have learned that if you have a pure heart and truly care about the person, the truth must be said. The goal is to transform the heart of the offender, not to make them want to run from the conversation and back to their sin.

If the person is in sin, they may get upset with you when you speak the truth. That's OK. However, that's why it is so important to show the other person what Scripture says, *not* your own opinion of what Scripture says. Too many times opinions are given based on or own understanding, not based on Scripture itself. Our own interpretation can make things worse and twist the truth. Open the book and read it directly from Scripture. Then there is freedom from who is right and who is wrong when you read the truth directly from God's Word. There have been times someone has said something to me I knew was not correct, but I chose to hold my tongue until I had a chance to check the Scripture myself.

Before you have the conversation, pray and then ask them first if you can get your Bible out to show them. If they say yes, they really do want to know the truth. If they are comfortable with allowing you to show them in the Bible, show them the Scripture and have them read what the Word says. There is life in the Word. God will speak for Himself so that you don't have to. Trust in God, knowing that His Word is true and let the Lord speak to their heart.

After all, God is the one who set up the divine appointment anyway. Be glad that you could be used as His instrument. Then it is time for the Lord to speak to them and set the captive free. "Then you will know the truth, and the truth will set you free" (John 8:32).

I want to go over this Scripture because it is one that people like to twist. To know the truth is what sets the captive free. You don't just know the information with some of your own added words from a memory of something you heard once or twice in a church service. You know the Scripture because you read it word for word.

The word *captive* refers to a person held in a lie or in confusion rooted in deception. But when the truth is given and that truth has been made known or understood, freedom takes place. That person is no longer held captive to deception. Then it is up to that person to be responsible with the wisdom given to them. They must understand that the Word of God is true and then choose to change the thoughts that affect their behavior or stay bound.

My friend Kimberly Howey told me something very important that I want to share with you. This wisdom literally changed my way of viewing someone's rights. She said, "The best gift God ever gave humans is free will, the right to choose. Don't ever go against someone's free will."

You may not like that they are choosing to not listen to you, and your intentions are probably noble, but you can't force someone to do or believe what you believe. If God won't force someone to believe or not believe, why should we try to make someone do something that is against their will to fit our own agenda? That's not free will, that's slavery and control. I learned a long time ago that the only person I can control is me. Trying to have an open discussion isn't about who is right and who is wrong. The goal behind the conversation is to show that person your point of view so they can understand where you are coming from.

Even if they understand why you think the way you think, it doesn't mean they will bend in that direction. That is why it is a disagreement. Maybe it will just take a move of God to help them surrender their will to His will.

I have learned that for some, "I'm sorry" are the most difficult words in our culture. Not just for adults but children, too, saying those words takes practice starting at a very young age. Basically, it's humbly taking responsibility for one's actions. Otherwise our behavior is because of pride, selfishness, and rebellion rooted in disobedience.

Arguments trying to force someone to say or do the right things are just not worth the stress. Sure, it would be nice to hear those words and for that person to understand where you are coming from, but remember, we live in a fallen world. Just know that there are always consequences for rebellion. Believe me, I know it's hard to watch someone making wrong choices, but sometimes that's the best way for people to learn on their own.

With that understood, it is still very important to spend time in prayer with God before and after you have a difficult conversation that might be confrontational or challenging. Ask God to give you His words not your own. If you plant a seed in someone's heart and they reject it, don't get discouraged, and don't give up on praying for that person.

God wants them set free, and He will use you and anyone else up for the task to accomplish what He set out to do. God is looking for those who want to be a willing partner in fulfilling His purposes for His kingdom. Keep praying that the Lord will open their eyes to the truth. I have learned that there are times and seasons for everything. Sometimes when we take a step back from the situation, things tend to work themselves out on their own without another word being said. When the door opens again for the conversation, stay on topic. No finger pointing. That only diverts the conversation from the purpose and turns it back to selfishness and pride.

Never, I mean, *never* get into an argument with the person about Scripture. That certainly does not end well! Being bold is not the same as arguing. Sometimes, saying less is more, and waiting for the right timing is the key to opening someone's eyes to the truth, even if that means removing yourself from the conversation until things cool down. If you can't talk in a civil manner, tell the person you need to step away for a little while until you can clear your thoughts. Then pray about the timing of the conversation. When the moment is right, get to the point and be done with it. Be strategic in the few but motivating words you want to say. Then stop!

Can you tell I have had practice at this? I'm not perfect, but I have gotten a whole lot better than I used to be. Thank You, Jesus!

Forgiveness is important as well. Just because that person may not understand or may be unhappy with you for what you feel is right, doesn't mean that you should carry their burden. We must be careful that our hearts don't become hardened. A hardened heart is where the enemy will try to get his foot in the door. That's not where you want to end up. "But if you do not forgive others their sins, your Father will not forgive your sins" (Matt. 6:15).

I truly believe God brings people into our sphere of influence so He can use us to help others. Remember, it is not about you, it is about Jesus and transforming the heart of His people into what the Lord wants them to be. And let's be honest with ourselves, it might be you or me who is wrong if we are not seeking the Word during the dispute. It is imperative to stay humble, keep your voice calm, and walk in love. The goal is to know the truth that will set us free, not to hold others or ourselves even more captive than we may already be. For instructions on God's way to handle disagreements read Matthew 18:15–20. "Follow God's example, therefore, as dearly loved children and walk in the way of love, just as Christ loved us and gave himself up for us as a fragrant offering and sacrifice to God" (Eph. 5:1–2).

Friend, go and be the light! Through you, God will show His love for His children. Be bold and walk in truth and love. Then let God do what only He can do best.

Big hugs,
Papa God and Ashley

Moses Out of the Water

Have you ever been reading a Scripture and something in it just jumps off the page at you? You may have read the same story over and over, and suddenly one passage or one word stands out, revealing a new revelation. I call those aha moments. My eyes usually get really big, and I get excited at what the Holy Spirit has just taught me. Hence, one of the reasons I wrote this book is to get you excited about the many treasures in the Word of God. The Word of God is so fascinating to me.

One night I was reading Exodus, chapters 1 and 2, the story of Moses, to my kids. I had never read the story of Moses with this revelation before, so I must share it with you, too! As I briefly narrate the event, the story picks up after Joseph had passed away, and a new pharaoh who did not know Joseph came to rule Egypt. The Hebrew population had grown, and Pharaoh became concerned that they were becoming too strong in numbers. His prideful attitude wanted to control the Hebrew people through slavery. Isn't that just how the enemy works? Satan is always trying to enslave God's beloved.

When slavery and brutality did not work, Pharaoh set up a decree for the Egyptian midwives to allow the baby girls to live, but to kill the newborn baby boys. The midwives, however, feared God and came up with an excuse that Hebrew women delivered too quickly, so they could not get to the birth in time to kill the baby boys. This infuriated Pharaoh, and he gave the order to throw all the newborn baby boys in the Nile River to die.

In Exodus chapter 2, Moses comes on the scene. His mother knew he was special when he was born, so she came up with a plan to put him in a basket and set him down in the reeds along the Nile River in hopes that God would protect her special child. Isn't it amazing how God always has a backup plan to defer the attacks and plans of the enemy?

Soon after Moses was placed in the river, the princess of Egypt came to the river to bathe. She heard the cry of a baby and sent her maidservant to bring her the child. Although Pharaoh's daughter recognized that the baby was a Hebrew child, she felt compassion for him, found a nursemaid (who was Moses' mother), and asked her to nurse her own son. Pharaoh's daughter later adopted Moses as her own. We all should pretty much know this story, but Exodus 2:10 hit me like a ton of bricks. "When the child grew older, she took him to Pharaoh's daughter and he became her son. She named him Moses, saying, 'I drew him out of the water'" (Ex. 2:10).

In my studies, I discovered that the princess named the child very specifically. She said she named him Moses because "she drew him out of the water" (Ex. 2:10). This was my aha moment. It was only the beginning of a revelation that the Holy Spirit was teaching me something new.

Scripture speaks of baptism as an outward proclamation that when we go down into the water, we die to our former self and come up as a new creation in Christ. The old man has passed away, and all things become new, revealing the new birth in Christ.

Before I go further into my point and fully unpack it for you, we know when his mother put him into the river, the baby Moses had a high chance of drowning, being eaten by a crocodile, or dying of starvation or dehydration. Basically, there was no hope for Moses! Pharaoh knew it, Moses' mom knew it, and the princess knew it. But Moses' mom trusted God because she somehow knew Moses was very special. Listen closely, even Satan knew this kid was special, and he wanted him dead. But God had another plan!

Moses, in the natural realm, was as good as dead based on the decree that the pharaoh had placed on the Hebrew people. My revelation was that when Moses was placed in the Nile River as a doomed boy, this was his former life. But God made a way through earthly royalty to change the outcome of this child's life and the lives of the Jewish people.

The princess raised Moses as her own, and eventually God used Moses to set his people free from slavery in Egypt, establish the law through the Ten Commandments, and lead the Israelites in the desert.

The fact that Moses went down into the water as a slave and was lifted out as royalty, is a metaphor for what happens to us when we give our lives to Jesus and are baptized. The Old Testament points to everything Christ would do for us, and in the New Testament, Christ fulfilled the law. Doesn't this revelation just set your feet to dancing and raise your hands high up in the air? Praise God!

This story sets the stage for what was to come through the life, death, and resurrection of Jesus Christ for His people. He is our royal priest who was, who is, and is still to come. Baptism in water is an outward expression of washing away the old and becoming a new creation in Christ. The old has passed away. Praise God that that old grime and filth is washed clean! There is something so miraculous about what happens when we are baptized. It's almost hard to explain in the natural realm what happens to us, not only on the outside but on the inside, in our spirit man. When I was baptized as an adult, my life changed. I can't explain exactly how, but I know it did. Every time I see people at church being baptized, I cry. It is just such an emotional experience for me to see.

My daughter once asked me, "Mom, why should we read a story that I have already read many times before?" First, it's not just about reading a story; it's about spending time with our Papa God and building a relationship with Him.

Second, the Holy Spirit will give you more and more revelation when you take the time to sit with Him and listen. God is full of new revelation. I think He gets more excited to teach us something new than we do when we receive it, just like any good parent does when our children figure something out that just changes their whole world as they know it.

So go read and reread those stories in the Bible. Ask the Holy Spirit to teach you something new before you start reading and thank Him for the time you have together. I promise He will meet you there right where you are and give you those aha moments, too.

Big hugs,
Papa God and Ashley

What Is Your Promised Land?

As I have gone through various life struggles, I have found myself feeling the need to reach out with my hands held high to our loving Father. Sometimes, in the middle of the chaos, that is all I can do. Like a child, I want to crawl up in Papa God's lap and have Him just hold me for a while.

Even though the tears may come, I know that He alone can comfort me. Scripture never said this life would come without trouble, but it does say that He is always with us. It is important to hold tight to our faith, knowing that God is a big God, and He knows the beginning to the end.

Even in the middle of the storm, I have found that it is important to not give up on my faith and the promises I have heard from the Lord. Listening to that still, small voice is so imperative. It may take going to a quiet place to truly hear Him. Once the words are clear, it is important to be obedient to what the Lord says, no matter how difficult His words may seem at that time. Often, I will write on a notepad or my journal what I have heard the Holy Spirit say to me. This way, I can go back and reflect on what He said later.

God wants more than anything to help His children in the difficult times of our lives, just like any loving father would. First, He wants to know if your heart is willing to trust Him and to listen to Him. "Trust in the Lord with all your heart and lean not on your own understanding; in all your ways submit to him, and he will make your paths straight" (Prov. 3:5–6).

There may be times in our lives God is saying to us: "Things are changing but it is for the better, and I want you to trust that I have this."

At times, I have had difficulty facing big changes. But I pressed through, knowing God is with me, and I can overcome anything the enemy planned for my destruction because my God will work out all things for those who trust Him. (See Rom. 8:28.)

When looking back on the course of my life, I can see the bigger picture and where God has led me to today. Even though, in the moment, I cannot see beyond the challenges, I know in my heart that God does. He already promised us in Hebrews 13:5 that He would never leave us or fail us.

I want to take you to the story in Joshua 1–5 when he was about to take the Israelites into the Promised Land. As we read this story, we know there were challenges along the way even when God told them they would take the land. It was up to Joshua to be obedient to the Lord and trust that God had his back. There were even giants in the Promised Land, and there were naysayers who were afraid to take the land because of these giants. But God is bigger than the giants in your promise, and God always keeps His promises. "No one will be able to stand against you all the days of your life. As I was with Moses, so I will be with you; I will never leave you nor forsake you" (Josh. 1:5).

My friend, you are not alone. God is for you. Things may not always end up the way we want them to, or we may not even understand why things are happening at that moment. But if you are listening to the

Lord, He will guide you. Trust that the outcome will be even better than what you could have imagined.

Keep believing and waiting on the Lord. In due time, He will lift you up and take you into the land He has promised you. Have faith and stand strong in the Lord. Don't look at the giants who seem so much bigger than you. Keep your eyes on Papa God, seek His will, and He will fight for you. Once you're finally in that Promised Land, praise God for all He has done and for all He still has planned for you.

Big hugs,
Papa God and Ashley

He Delights in Me

Can you imagine what God's face looks like when we do something that pleases Him? I can almost see Him watching us as we walk around throughout our day. He smiles when He sees us run to open a door for an elderly woman struggling to walk. There is this knowing in our heart that she is hoping someone will be around to help her. Or what about when we see a homeless person holding a sign on the side of the road in the scorching summer heat of 98+ degrees? The Holy Spirit somehow sends us across this person's path for a reason. We look down in our cup holder, and we realize we just came from the gas station where we grabbed a cold bottle of water. We roll down our car window to hand it to the guy while he is standing there dying of thirst and just about overheated.

Maybe it's while we are driving and singing our little hearts out worshiping God with one of our favorite songs on the radio. I know it may sound silly to you, but I like to sometimes pretend I am having my own concert with the angels singing to God! Even if I am off key a little, He doesn't care, and He just smiles at me, knowing I am singing to Him.

I am sure He smiles at whatever we are doing at the time that pleases Him. If anything, it sure is comforting to know that He is always watching over us and directing our path. Because I know the Lord delights in His children, I really do believe God and His angels sing with us. "The Lord your God is with you, the Mighty Warrior who saves. He will take great delight in you; in his love he will no longer rebuke you, but will rejoice over you with singing" (Zeph. 3:17).

I know for a fact that angels sing with us while we are worshiping the Lord. Although I have not always heard them singing in every church service, I have been in a praise and worship service where many of us have heard the voices of angels singing along with us. It was the most amazing experience! We were singing the song, "It Is Well with My Soul." Once I knew they were there, I stopped singing for a little bit just to hear their voices. It was so beautiful and exciting to know they were worshiping God with us.

It's in those moments of worship that I receive many revelations from the Holy Spirit. I recall one of those days I wrote a poem and a prayer to the Lord. My heart was so full of joy in that moment. I feel honored that I can share my poem with you. It is about how the Lord delights in us when we love on Him and when we do those things for others that please Him. I hope you enjoy it.

As You walk with me, Lord, throughout my day, I know that You
    are with me.
Your love dances over me in a great celebration of song.
Your angels surround me, even when I may not realize they are there.
You set them charge over me, and they protect me from all danger.
You, Lord, comfort my soul. I focus on keeping my thoughts fixed
    on You.
I may not know what comes around each corner, but You, Lord,
    have a bird's-eye view of my path.

You see far above every situation. Your plans for me are good and
to prosper me.

Speak to me and let me hear Your voice loud and clear, Lord.

Tune my ears to Your voice. I am yet a sheep, and You are my Great
Shepherd.

All of my hope is in You, Papa.

I do not want to miss You, Lord, and what great treasures You have
in store for me today.

I can't wait to see all the wonderful surprises You have thought of
just for me.

May Your joy overflow in me because of Your greatness. You are so
magnificent!

Shower me with Your glory, oh, Lord!

You delight in me and I delight in You. Let this light shine for all
to see.

Thank you, Lord, for Your love for me.

We were created to worship and love God. This is why our bodies
react to the presence of the Holy Spirit. So sing, cry, and raise your hands
in admiration to the One who delights in you. Watch and see how He
loves on you in return. There is no greater expression of love then the
time spent in the intimacy with Papa God.

Big hugs,
Papa God and Ashley

The Valley of the Shadow of Death

Dying to ourselves isn't the easy way, but it is the better way. It is God's way. Dying to ourselves means putting our own wants and needs aside and seeking what God wants for us instead. It is surrendering all things in our lives to Him. Surrendering to the will of God can be a challenge at times when we are going through what the Word calls the valley or an extremely low point in our lives.

The psalmist David had a wonderful relationship with God. In Psalm 23, he reflected on his experience when he was younger. Before David became king, he was a shepherd in the fields. A shepherd must be strong, attentive, nurturing, and on guard always. There is much danger, and sheep have many predators. Sheep are vulnerable and frightened animals, but they are good followers of their masters. Because of their vulnerability, they are completely dependent on their masters for comfort, provision, and protection. The shepherd David is describing in Psalm 23 is Jesus. "My sheep listen to my voice; I know them, and they follow me" (John 10:27).

As a shepherd tending to the needs of his sheep, there were times he had to transfer his sheep from one location to another to get to better pastures for grazing and often for safety. There were times they would have to go through uncharted territory or rough terrain to get to better pastures. At any sight or sound of danger, the sheep would become afraid, but they knew and trusted the shepherd so they followed him even when they had to go through valleys that were scary. The sheep need their shepherd; apart from him, they could die.

> The Lord is my shepherd, I lack nothing. He makes me lie down in green pastures, he leads me beside quiet waters, he refreshes my soul. He guides me along the right paths for his name's sake. Even though I walk through the darkest valley, I will fear no evil, for you are with me; your rod and your staff, they comfort me. You prepare a table before me in the presence of my enemies. You anoint my head with oil; my cup overflows. Surely your goodness and love will follow me all the days of my life, and I will dwell in the house of the Lord forever. (Ps. 23)

I love reading Psalm 23 when I am sitting nice and snug in my safe living room. Going through the valley of the shadow of death sounds so pretty, on paper, and when life is easy. In real life, when you're personally going through the valley, it's a different story.

When life is tough, I can empathize with these sheep. The world seems to be spinning out of control, and everywhere you turn, it seems like anything and everything that can go wrong, goes wrong. Then there are thoughts that seem like they won't stop tormenting our minds, and all we want to do is run back to our safe place. Those shadows in the valley seem larger than life. At times, they seem like they may even win and keep us in the darkness. But that is why keeping our eyes on Jesus in the valley is so crucial.

God gave me a vision of this dark valley that I want to share with you. The Holy Spirit showed me that the shadows hovering over you are not reality when your faith is in action. With God, they are only shadows and are not real. These are only a tactic of the enemy to try and intimidate you and cause you to panic.

Looking at the circumstances and danger will never get us out of the valley quicker. It will only keep us there longer. There's a line from a song my daughter Rachael used to sing when she was little: "You can't go over it, you can't go under it, and you'll have to go through it!"

Even though we must go through the valley, it doesn't mean God's not with us.

He is.

It doesn't mean He does not care.

He does.

He is saying, "Keep your eyes on Me, and we will get to the other side together. Do you trust Me?"

The answer is, "Yes! Yes, Lord, I do, and I certainly don't want to go alone."

The valley can feel uncertain and even scary at times. There have been times I have said, "No God, I don't want to go through this place in my life. I know there's a reason, but I am scared, Lord. This is the battle I have been dreading. Yet it's here and there's no avoiding it." My heart has cried out to God in the middle of the valley, "I know it's time to put on my big kid pants, Papa God, and go through this valley. And I am so glad You are with me."

If we trust God and have Him walk with us through it, when we look back from the other side, it will all make sense in the end. The Lord is saying, "Don't let the shadows scare you; the greener pastures aren't far off. There's a reason, and I want to show you the way through. Come on with Me and be strong. I've got this, remember? Those shadows are not going to harm you. Though your flesh will want to panic over the circumstances, stay focused on the light. Though it may seem dim at this moment, keep your eyes on Me. With Me by your side, do not fear. I am with you and we will see the victory! I am God, and with Me *all* things are possible. Ready? Here, grab my hand. Do you see this rod in My other hand? I will not allow anything to harm you. Trust me." "Even though I walk through the darkest valley, I will fear no evil, for you are with me; your rod and your staff, they comfort me" (Ps. 23:4).

I once heard a sermon about what the rod in the shepherd's hand was for. It was used for multiple things. The first was a way to reach out and gently guide the sheep around him in the direction they needed to go. It was also used as a weapon against predators. The shepherd would use it to smack predators hard to scare them off because they were trying to kill his sheep. "You prepare a table before me in the presence of my enemies. You anoint my head with oil; my cup overflows" (Ps. 23:5).

In that same sermon, it was disclosed that flies would land on the faces of the sheep and lay eggs inside their nostrils. The eggs hatch, and the maggots crawl up inside the brains of the sheep and drive them crazy, so much so that the sheep would bang their heads against a wall because the maggots were crawling all around. The shepherd would use soothing oils to pour over their heads, and it would trickle down the face of the sheep to sooth them and ward off the flies.

As bizarre as this sounds, doesn't this description give you a good example of how it feels when life is hard and the attacks are coming from every angle? The shepherd is their advocate, protector, and source of comfort. When we get over the panic of the situation at hand, that is when God can move in our lives and calm us back down in an effort to move His sheep forward. That is when we can walk safely with Him through that valley.

If you are in the valley, get your Bible out and seek the Lord. Singing always brings joy, and those shadows are only shadows of fear and doubt, and they can't stand the joy of the Lord. When we praise God around them, they start to fade away. God's goodness and love are what cause us to follow Him.

Let the peace of God go with you all the way through to the other side. His grace is the anointing oil you need to walk peacefully through the circumstances of life.

Trust God through it. God promised in His Word that He is the Great Shepherd, and if we love and trust Him, the journey will be worth it in the end. Yes, there are lessons to be learned, but we must let go of the way we want to go through those valleys. Remember, He knows the way through it. God will restore all that the enemy has tried to take from Papa God's beloved.

Big hugs,
Papa God and Ashley

To Know God

One morning, the Lord brought me to the book of Job. I must admit that I had tried to read this book in the past, but it was one of those books that were really hard for me to read, not because it's difficult, but because it can be depressing. At times, Job's story is not a fun one to read, although all stories have a happy ending with God, and the story always points to His love for us.

You see, Job was a man after God's heart. Scripture says that he loved God and turned from evil. With that said, you know Job will go through a test to determine his love and devotion. To summarize the story, Satan asked God if Job was truly devoted to Him. If so, Satan wanted to test Job for his loyalty to God, and God allowed it.

Then the LORD said to Satan, "Have you considered my servant Job? There is no one on earth like him; he is blameless and upright, a man who fears God and shuns evil." "Does Job fear God for nothing?" Satan replied. "Have you not put a hedge around him and his household and everything he has? You have blessed the work of his hands so that his flocks and herds are spread throughout the land. But now stretch out your hand and strike everything he has, and he will surely curse you to your face." The LORD said to Satan, "Very well, then, everything he has is in your power, but on the man himself, do not lay a finger." (Job 1:8–12)

Job went through some very tragic circumstances during this time in his life, losing all that he had. To make matters even worse, his foolish friends tried to give him advice on why they felt he was going through all these terrible things. Some of their advice was OK, but most of the time, they were only speaking for themselves and accusing Job of things he never did or thought. Time and time again, Job defended his position, and although he did not fully understand why these things were happening to him, he never cursed or blamed God.

Job did, however, start to question God, which I think is a normal reaction for someone who truly loves the Lord and is trying to understand. (I know that I have been in this position a time or two myself). Most people would have given up on their faith in God in the middle of the trial, but not Job! He continued to stand firm in his beliefs.

Job pleaded with God for answers, and God spoke to him in the most unlikely way. Instead of answering all of Job's questions (because they were irrelevant), He spoke to Job about His own creation and authority. God used Job's lack of knowledge to explain to Job who He is.

You see, God's ways are higher than our ways. He created this universe and all that is in it out of nothing through His wisdom and His words.

The LORD Speaks
Then the LORD spoke to Job out of the storm. He said: "Who is this that obscures my plans with words without knowledge? Brace yourself like a man; I will question you, and you shall answer me. Where were you when I laid the earth's foundation? Tell me, if you understand. Who marked off its dimensions? Surely you know! Who stretched a measuring line across it? On what were its footings set, or who laid its

cornerstone—while the morning stars sang together and all the angels shouted for joy? Who shut up the sea behind doors when it burst forth from the womb, when I made the clouds its garment and wrapped it in thick darkness, when I fixed limits for it and set its doors and bars in place, when I said, 'This far you may come and no farther; here is where your proud waves halt?'" (Job 38:1–11)

This response from God always amazes me. He basically asks Job, "Where were you when I laid the foundations of the earth?" God created everything without asking advice from anyone. He just thought of the ocean, told it where to start and where to end, and it was.

Job's friends made matters even worse; they could sit there and judge Job all they wanted, but they never truly gave him the answers he was seeking. Questioning God and His reasons shows that Job was confused! Has this ever happened to you? You trust God but others come along and worsen the situation. They judged Job without knowing the answers, too. They only made assumptions of why Job was going through complete hell.

Only God is the true Judge, and He holds all the answers. Sometimes, we think we know all and want to try to explain the answers to life by coming up with our own conclusions.

Again, God is saying, "Where were you when the morning stars sang together and all the angels shouted for joy? How can you question things you just don't know yet or understand?" Sounds logical, right?

Honestly, God is the answer, and He is the One who knows all things. He wasn't trying to condemn Job or make him feel foolish. Remember, God loves us. He is very strategic in how He plans things out. And because Job stood strong in his faith, by the end of his trial, God restored his life to even better than before!

God will bring us to a place to seek His wisdom and mercy so that we can draw closer to Him. He wants us to know Him better because He loves us. But He also wants us to choose Him and His ways. He wants to be a part of our life's journey, to walk with us and show us things we do not know or yet understand. He's not hiding things from us with the intention of harming us. I believe God longs to show us new things, things He created just for our enjoyment.

Honestly, I think God is so creative, and I joyfully proclaim that He's a bit of a show-off! If you think that is funny, go look outside at the night sky and try to count the stars to see what I mean. I bet you can't even come close to the actual number in just a few feet of your visual view. Or even better, count the blades of grass in your front yard. On the other hand, don't. You might look a little silly to your neighbors, and your three best friends might have a talking with you. I am joking of course, but I think you get my point. God is pretty amazing and magnificent! His grandeur is unmatched and incomprehensible even by the wisest scientists. God goes beyond what our imagination can even comprehend. Scripture says that He knows all the stars by name. (See Ps. 147:4.)

Think about that for a second. For every inch of stars we see, there are billions of stars and other galaxies inside clusters of stars, and He knows each of them by name. If He knows all of them by name, don't you think He knows your name and loves you that much more? It makes me feel very special that the God who created the universe and beyond wants to know me personally and listens to my every thought and word. He is so amazing that He can listen and speak to every single person on the planet at the exact same time! That's mind-blowing! This is because He is omnipotent, omniscience, and omnipresence. He is all-powerful, all-knowing and all-present. If we think even for a second that we know it all, we are wrong.

Going back, my favorite part of Job's story is after he repented for thinking he knows all that God knows and for trying to figure out everything by his own limited understanding, the storms of his life had passed. Job makes the most astounding statement that just touched my heart. He told God that he not only knew *of* God, he now *knew* Him. He stayed with Job even in the worst times of his life and taught him who God really is and who Job was to God. The outcome was they had a relationship with each other they did not have before. Read what Job said to God:

Job speaks
Then Job replied to the LORD: "I know that you can do all things; no purpose of yours can be thwarted. You asked, 'Who is this that obscures my plans without knowledge?' Surely, I spoke of things I did not understand, things too wonderful for me to know. You said, 'Listen now, and I will speak; I will question you, and you shall answer me.' My ears had heard of you but now my eyes have seen you. Therefore, I despise myself and repent in dust and ashes." (Job 42:1–6)

That statement from Job to God gives me goose bumps. My interpretation of his response to God is, "Who am I to understand all things?" Even when we don't understand why God allows things to happen to us, stay the course. In the end, God will always cause us to triumph through trusting in Him. Job only thought he knew God before; now his eyes were wide open to God as the Creator, the God who created all things for our good. The tough times in our lives make us stronger and help us to understand the bigger picture of life beyond ourselves.

My heart cries out to know God more than I can imagine or think. He is so wonderful that my mind cannot begin to comprehend how truly wonderful He is. Like Job, I am learning more and more every day about who He is and who I am to Him.

God has great plans for you. In those hard times, let God be God, lean into Him, and trust Him. No matter what happens in our lives, He knows your story from before He laid the foundations of the earth, and He had you in mind when He thought of your time and place in history. He even knew the choices you would make way before we were on this earth. Remember you still have free will, the right to choose, but He still knows you, and He loves you very much.

I admit that I have been in Job's shoes more than once in my life. I have questioned God's motives and begged for the answers to my life's most difficult situations. In those moments, God showed me that I would learn something to help me see the bigger picture so that I could be relatable to you and others.

The good news is that even though the trails of life hurt, I am thankful for the opportunity to have been through them because I, too, don't just want to know of God, I want to *know* Him and His plans for me. I want to see those miracles in my life. To do this, we need to be close enough to Him that we hear His voice loud and clear. We must know Him intimately and know that His Word is true and turn our hearts back to Him.

Please recite this declaration with me today; ask to know God, not just to know of Him and to trust Him through the storms of life.

Prayer

Thank You, God, for the times in my life I did not understand because those were the times I learned the most about who You are and how much I needed You. I confess that I have sought out wisdom from others who do not know Your plans for me. I am so glad that You are God and that You hold all the answers for me. I ask You to give me the strength I need and to show me who You are. Walk with me through the trials and reveal all the answers to get me through to the other side.

Your plans are far above my plans and thoughts. I know Your blessings for me will be greater than what I had before because I trust You. Restore my life and bring me closer to You, Lord. I don't just want to know of You; I want to know and see You in all aspects of my life, Lord.

In Jesus' name, amen.

Big hugs,
Papa God and Ashley

God Wants Your Heart

There is so much controversy about tithing but not too much for those who don't have a problem with it! The controversy comes from the people who don't understand biblical principles and why Christ-followers are required to tithe.

I read something pertaining to tithing from Peter Chapman, founder of topverses.com, and I thought it was worth sharing with you. Chapman writes, "Here is a reminder about how the economy of God works. It's like the laws of physics, except this one applies to life. We receive by giving." "One person gives freely, yet gains even more; another withholds unduly but comes to poverty" (Prov. 11:24).

The kingdom of God is a governmental system. God governs by planting a seed and receiving a harvest. Because He is the giver of life, tithing is set up so that when we give, we receive something even better from God that is fruitful and multiplies. "As long as the earth endures, seedtime and harvest, cold and heat, summer and winter, day and night will never cease" (Gen. 8:22).

One weekend, my daughter Reagan worked by doing household chores for some money. She was about eight years old at the time. The next day was Sunday, and I told her, "Honey, you need to give God 10 percent of what you earned." I explained that this is what God requires of us to do with the money we earn. "It's our first fruits that go back to Him, so that He can continue to bless us and we can, in turn, bless others." Because of her heart to please God, she understood, and she gave 10 percent in the offering plate the next day. I could tell that it was somewhat of a test for her to see if what I was saying was true.

That next weekend, my family and I went to the fairgrounds to see a concert. Like any concert, there were hundreds of people everywhere. We were walking toward the amphitheater and Reagan looked down on the ground and noticed a twenty-dollar bill someone had dropped. She immediately got very excited and screamed, "I found twenty dollars!" Then a guy who was walking near us came close and tried to take her twenty dollars. We knew it was not his since he was walking behind us and had also just come from the parking lot like we did. We knew he just wanted to take advantage of what Reagan had found.

He saw my husband and I were nearby, and he left. Do you see what happened? When we tithe, God will also protect the gift He intends to give us as a reward.

Once the guy left, Reagan was very excited and said, "Mom, God took care of me and gave me more since I tithed at church last Sunday!"

If you are not a tither, I know what you might be thinking. "That was just a coincidence. Anyone can find money on the ground." But wait, there's more.

The next Sunday, Reagan tithed 10 percent of her twenty dollars. The following weekend we went over to my friend Mary's house and played a game of bingo where the winner could win some money. Every game Reagan played, she won the money. After this happened about four or five times, everyone started joking with Reagan saying she wasn't allowed to play anymore because she had won too much and had too much favor. Maybe they didn't quite understand what favor this was, but I did. It was the favor of God! Remember, she was only about eight years old at the time. She had never played that game before and to constantly win was pretty impressive. Needless to say, we all had a lot of fun, and Reagan learned a big lesson on tithing again.

God does not need your money. What He wants is your heart and for you to trust Him with your money. When churches ask for money, it's not God asking you to give because He needs it. The earth is the Lord's and everything in it. (See Ps. 24:1, 1 Cor. 10:26.) He created everything; He doesn't need our help. He is YAWEH, which means *God is our provider and our constant help in need.* He wants to know that you love Him and others more than what is in your wallet. God looks at our hearts, our intentions, and for a willingness to give as an investment that leads others into a life changing relationship with Him. Since God is a giver, He is faithful to give more than we can imagine.

Satan will always try to steal from you, and he will make you think you shouldn't tithe, blocking us from God's blessings. Where God is involved, He freely gives back to those who honor Him with their tithes. Besides, we can't take it with us when these bodies pass away! Plus, our government requires way more than the small amount God is asking to freely give. Jesus said it best. "Then Jesus said to them, 'Give back to Caesar what is Caesar's and to God what is God's'" (Mark 12:17).

Life is about serving God and bringing others into the kingdom of God, which is love, life, and freedom. God designed His plans for us based on seed time and harvest. We reap the harvest of what we plant. If we plant roses we're going to grow rose bushes not wheat thistles. Churches use the tithe money to keep the doors open so that others who need Jesus can come. This is the harvest of souls that is eternal. Just like what Peter Chapman said earlier in this chapter, "Tithing applies to our everyday lives," when we give, we receive. God set it up that way on purpose. God is a giver of life, and His goal is to give to His children abundantly. Jesus said it like this. "The thief comes only to steal and kill and destroy; I have come that they may have life, and have it to the full" (John 10:10).

There are two separate things: tithing that God requires and offerings. God cares about both.

There's just something about how we feel when we give a love offering to someone else in need. It's a morale booster. When you see that big smile on someone's face, you know you have done something that made their day. Or you see that person start to cry because this one act of generosity answered their prayers.

Of course, it doesn't always have to be just money that we give in our offerings. Offerings are gifts of gratitude and respect for the gift of life, itself. It could be your time as a volunteer, a listening ear, or a kind act of service. I believe that one act of kindness gives back to us. It gives us a sense of kindness, accomplishment, and worthiness. Others may see it, and then it becomes contagious! An example is when someone opens the door to a building for the person behind them and that person opens the door for the next, and so on it goes on down the line to the next person entering in. "Give, and it will be given to you. A good measure, pressed down, shaken together and running over, will be poured into your lap. For with the measure you use, it will be measured to you" (Luke 6:38).

I love to give without the expectancy of anything in return more than I love to receive. It gives me a pep in my step and a smile on my face. If it gives us all of this, imagine what our Papa God is thinking when he sees His children giving the way He gives to us? I know it warms His heart and that He is proud of His children when we show His love to others. It gives Him great joy.

Bring the whole tithe into the storehouse, that there may be food in my house. "Test me in this," says the Lord Almighty, "and see if I will not throw open the floodgates of heaven and pour out so much blessing that there will not be room enough to store it. I will prevent pests from devouring your crops, and the vines in your fields will not drop their fruit before it is ripe," says the Lord Almighty. (Mal. 3:10–11)

Go try it, and you will see! Tithing is the only place in Scripture where God says to test Him in this. When you give with your whole heart, the joy of the Lord and His blessings will overflow into your own life and pour out into the lives of others.

Big hugs,
Papa God and Ashley

Dark Clouds

Early one morning, I was on the phone with a dear friend of mine, Denise. We were having a conversation about the sky. She was driving to work, and I was sitting in my office. As I looked out my office window, I could see it was a dark and gloomy morning. It was also cold outside that day, and it was right around the time the sun was coming up. The clouds were pitch black, but the most brilliant colors of orange and yellow ever so slightly glazed the top of those dark clouds.

I really admire Denise as a mom, friend, and a mighty woman of God. Every conversation with Denise is so calm, and she is kind-spirited. But more importantly, her words are powerful! I love spending time listening to her wisdom and her love for the Lord.

As we were both looking at the sky, we were talking about those times in our lives that seem dark and lonely. You know, those times you feel like you can't hear from God because of difficult circumstances? These circumstances can be overwhelming, and the feelings of hopelessness take over the voice of God. On this day, I had felt the attacks of the enemy on my moral values and beliefs, and I was struggling with feelings of defeat.

I'll never forget this exact moment because as we were talking, she said the most profound statement. She said, "Those dark clouds in the sky, Ashley, are the clouds that reflect the Son with the glory of the Lord."

Thinking about her statement, I had an epiphany from the Lord. He said, "Just because the clouds in our lives look dark and scary doesn't mean that I'm not behind them saying look a little closer. Can you see My brilliant light in these dark times? Get ready, My beloved; you're about to see the sun break through!"

> Dear friends, do not be surprised at the fiery ordeal that has come on you to test you, as though something strange were happening to you. But rejoice inasmuch as you participate in the sufferings of Christ, so that you may be overjoyed when his glory is revealed. If you are insulted because of the name of Christ, you are blessed, for the Spirit of glory and of God rests on you. (1 Peter 4:12–14)

Sometimes we should look a little harder to see what Papa God is about to do in those dark times. He is preparing us for something far greater than what we can see in that moment. Don't allow the devil to take your focus off the glory of God. Even in the darkest of times, God has great plans to see you through to the next chapter in your life and know that He is about to uncover them for everyone to see more clearly.

It is almost humorous how the enemy tries to use those close to us, and even those who may not know us, to attack our character and our beliefs. The enemy wants nothing more than to get us off course and to waiver in the truth. Scripture says to count it all joy when you feel persecuted because your reward is in heaven. (See Matt. 5:12.)

Realizing that this is a tactic of the enemy, I try to see past the persecution of those who don't know the awesome God we serve. I realize that it's an honor because it shows me that I am doing something right for God's kingdom, and it has the enemy frustrated and angry. This just makes me want to keep doing what I am doing because it pleases my

Lord. Just maybe those voices of rejection for my beliefs are still breaking through those walls of defiance of the Word of God in that person. The wall is still up, but slowly but surely the truth of God's Word is chipping away and making progress.

And wouldn't you know it, soon after I hung up the phone with Denise, the sun pushed through those clouds, and it was a beautiful day. Those dark clouds were an afterthought, and the day brought many blessings.

In these writings to you, it is my hope that you are drawing closer to Papa God like never before, and that your relationship with Him is alive and well. I pray something is taking root in you that cannot be uprooted.

I want to close this chapter with words from the apostle Paul to the church in Philippi. This prayer was his heart's desire for his friends, and this is my heart back to you. "And this is my prayer: that your love may abound more and more in knowledge and depth of insight, so that you may be able to discern what is best and may be pure and blameless for the day of Christ, filled with the fruit of righteousness that comes through Jesus Christ—to the glory and praise of God" (Phil. 1:9–11).

Be blessed and keep looking up. Your breakthrough is coming, just keep your eyes on the Son. May the Spirit of glory and of God rest on you!

Big hugs,
Papa God and Ashley

The Dance

One morning, as I was getting ready for my day, the song, "He Is with You" by Mandisa, came on my playlist. As I was listening closely to the lyrics of this song, I could imagine all the different scenarios of life that each and every one of us has had to face or may face in the future. There, in the middle of the song, I was reminded of this fallen world and how much words can truly hurt to the core.

I know this is going to sound cheesy, but I started to imagine what it would be like to dance with Jesus. One day when this world has passed away, we will finally see our Lord face to face. But until then, we feel and hear Him in our spirit man and through the actions of others.

In this moment, I could imagine Him saying, "My child, may I have this dance?"

My answer is, "Yes, Papa, please take the lead. I will follow Your every step."

When I was a little girl and my dad and I were listening to some music, he asked me if I would like to dance. Like a gentleman, he stood up in front of me and did a slight bow with his head down, holding his left hand behind his back with his right hand extended to me. Then my daddy showed me how to step up on his feet and how to hold my arms out as he grabbed my hands to dance. Round and round we would go in circles and step back and forth to the music. It was so much fun! It reminded me of Cinderella dancing with her Prince.

Here's a secret: I remembered the steps with my earthly father, I postured myself in the waltzing stance, put my arms and hands up in an elegant pose, and just went for it! In my bathroom, I danced and imagined I was in a grand ballroom waltzing around with Jesus! Yes, I did! I told you I was going to be cheesy.

As I did this, I reflected on the past and present emotional pain I have endured, while tears filled my eyes—all of this while in my Papa God's arms. It's such a safe place to be, yet freeing at the same time. I thought of all the people in this world, specifically those who do not know how much God truly loves them. I thought of all the people who do love God but can't understand or know how to follow His lead. They are so wrapped up in religious rules that they miss the relationship with God.

Although we cannot physically see our Lord in front of us, or in this case dancing with us, He is forever there. He knows the pain and sees the injustice going on, and He feels the hurt deep down inside.

As the song went on, my heart raced with the love and compassion He has for His children. I really hope you can see past the silliness of my story and see the heart of God in it for you.

I encourage you to find this song or any song that you can connect with Papa God and listen to it. While you listen to the words, let the Lord lead you in your emotional healing. Don't walk away from the dance without giving Him the chance to touch your heart.

Don't worry about feeling silly because it's not being silly, it is really being vulnerable before God. King David danced before God, and David had the most amazing relationship with Him. Because of his genuine love for God, David was highly favored and blessed. David was a mighty warrior, and he still had enough sense to be vulnerable before God.

"Wearing a linen ephod, David was dancing before the Lord with all his might, while he and all Israel were bringing up the ark of the Lord with shouts and the sound of trumpets" (2 Sam. 6:14–15).

Dance like David did, and dance like no one is watching!

God is saying, "May I have this dance?"

Are you ready? Step up on Papa God's feet and just dance!

Big hugs,
Papa God and Ashley

Thorn in My Side

Before I read 2 Corinthians, chapters 10 through 12, I wondered what the thorn in Paul's side actually was. I have heard many views on this, and I have my own understanding as well. I am sure you may have your opinion based on your teachings. However, I don't think Paul or the Holy Spirit wanted to be secretive about this thorn. There is a reason and a lesson in these letters Paul wrote to the church in Corinth for us to understand. To realize what Paul means, let's start at 2 Corinthians 12:6–8:

> *Even if I should choose to boast*, I would not be a fool, because I would be speaking the truth. But I refrain, so no one will think more of me than is warranted by what I do or say, or because of these *surpassingly great revelations*. Therefore, in order to keep me from becoming conceited, I was given *a thorn* in my flesh, *a messenger of Satan, to torment me.* Three times I pleaded with the Lord to take it away from me. (2 Cor. 12:6–8 emphasis added)

Let's begin dissecting this together. First, Paul was trying to keep himself humble and not sound boastful or conceited. He had spent a lot of time with people of the church in Corinth and he wrote two letters to mentor and lead them to Christ. We know this even from this passage because he mentioned all the surpassing great revelations he has experienced with God, but he knew all the credit goes to God and not himself. Then Paul refers to the thorn as a messenger of Satan sent to torment him. Based on the facts leading up to this portion of Scripture, we see that Paul was facing spiritual warfare because he made it very clear that a messenger of Satan was sent to torment him. Three times He asked God to take away this torment, but God had another plan for Paul.

Now let's break this down so we can fully understand this plan. I want to start with what God is showing me through this verse. Growing up, I heard people say things like, "That one is a thorn in my side." This means that someone is causing them grief. This person has caused some sort of frustration, and their actions are digging into the other person's emotions and affecting their thoughts and life by their stubbornness or disobedience. In essence, that person has become a roadblock or is exposed as being a blockhead! I know that sounds funny but stay with me. Can you see that this messenger is a person?

To confirm this revelation, I decided to look what a "thorn in the side" means by the definition and example. Definition: someone or something that continually causes problems for you: Money problems have been a thorn in our side since the day we got married. Health inspectors are a thorn in the side of most restaurants.[5]

I encourage you to read all of 2 Corinthians 12. You will see that Paul was venting his frustrations in a letter to the people in the church of Corinth before he returned to them for the third time. He was saying that before he comes back, he wants to correct them in writing so that

---

5   http://dictionary.cambridge.org/us/dictionary/english/thorn-in-your-side

he would not have to deal with this issue again. So again, this is a big clue that the thorn in Paul's side was *people* coming against him.

Have you ever experienced people coming against you whom you have had multiple conversations with, and in these conversations, you try to reason with them about a conflict between you? I am sure you are thinking of someone right now and how nothing you have said previously seems to stick in their minds. You have told them the truth hoping they would change their minds toward some misconduct, but they don't get it. That is when you may have resorted to writing down your feelings in a letter expecting they will read what you have to say. The purpose of the letter is to remove the blockade to gain mutual understanding and move forward. The letter seems a simple solution because you know they are not listening to you. Oh, they say they hear you, but your point is not registering in their brains because they continue to disagree with you when it is plain to see that they are in the wrong or doing the wrong things that are harmful to their growth toward maturity.

The people in Corinth were being stubborn toward Paul's message of the gospel. A letter was written to discontinue a conversation that was going nowhere verbally. Based on this letter, Paul was dealing with the people who are going back to their pre-salvation patterns and listening to the false teachers of that day. In 2 Corinthians 2:17 and 11:13, we see that Paul knew these false teachers well since he was educated by them, and they were also some of the leaders who may have tried to kill him. Read Chapters 10 and 11 to see this for yourself.

Now let's go back to Paul complaining to God. He explained that he has complained to God three times hoping that He would release him from these people or "thorns." I assume it had to be a very tough situation to want to walk away from people who aren't listening and aren't appreciating all that he had sacrificed for them. But God is a merciful God, and He loved the people He sent Paul to teach just as much as He loved Paul. Here is God's answer to Paul when he wanted out of this torment. "But he said to me, 'My grace is sufficient for you, for my power is made perfect in weakness.' Therefore, I will boast all the more gladly about my weaknesses, so that Christ's power may rest on me" (2 Cor. 12:9).

To paraphrase, Paul continues to tell the people of Corinth that he has weaknesses, too, but he will boast in those weaknesses because when he is made weak in his own struggles, Christ is working through him and making him strong.

Don't you learn from your mistakes? I have definitely learned some tough lessons by messing up, but when I learn the truth, these mistakes are what make me wiser even more.

Now let's go over the "thorns" in his side as Paul lists them. I really want you to see this so we can fully understand what Paul is saying. "That is why, for Christ's sake, I delight in weaknesses, in *insults*, in *hardships*, in *persecutions*, in *difficulties*. For when I am weak, then I am strong" (2 Cor. 12:10 emphasis added). Paul goes even deeper into the thorns who are causing the divide between them later in chapter 12. So I would like to dig deeper into this thorn. Pun intended! But seriously, have you ever experienced any of this? I am sure if you are in ministry, a teacher of any sort, or a parent, you will be able to relate to Paul.

> For I am afraid that when I come I may not find you as I want you to be, and you may not find me as you want me to be. I fear that there may be *discord, jealousy, fits of rage, selfish ambition, slander, gossip, arrogance* and *disorder*. I am afraid that when I come again my God will humble me before you, and I will be grieved over many who have sinned earlier and have not repented of the *impurity, sexual sin* and *debauchery* in which they have indulged. (2 Cor. 12:20–21 emphasis added)

Can you now see now why Paul was so frustrated, and can you see the thorn in his side? Doesn't it sound like these rebellious people are thorns?

The thorns are digging into his side, trying to come against everything he is trying to teach them. It is Satan's attempt to stop the move of the Holy Spirit to change lives from a sinful nature to a godly nature.

Listen, I've been there and even done that to people myself. I've had people who love and care about me correct me, and I have put up an attitude and dug deeper into the side of that person. Trust me, when children grow up and have their own kids, they go back to their God-fearing parents and finally tell them how awesome they are. Yes, you know it's true.

With that said, here is where my revelation comes in. But first, let's swing back around and look at God's response to Paul again after he complained three times and wanted to head for the hills. Paul wanted to run as far away as he could get from the people of Corinth. It kind of reminds me of Jonah's story. "But he said to me, 'My grace is sufficient for you, for my power is made perfect in weakness.' Therefore, I will boast all the more gladly about my weaknesses, so that Christ's power may rest on me" (2 Cor. 12:9).

God is saying, "Paul, we've got this. Go back, as I am with you. So don't get so prideful because we have been down 'Straight Street' before, you and Me." (Hold onto this thought; God is about to blow your mind.) "It's about *Me*, not about you, Paul. I want you to rest in My grace for these people. You have a job to do for Me. Don't get your feelings hurt. These attacks are only the enemy coming at you."

I am paraphrasing all of this, of course, but you get the point. So get this, based on my experience with spiritual warfare and reading about Paul's life, God was reminding Paul of who he used to be and what he has overcome through Christ in this response from God. At one point in Paul's life, he wasn't a good guy. He was very prideful and arrogant and thought he knew it all. He was well educated but a total and complete jerk. Paul was called Saul prior to his conversion to faith in Christ. Saul was a religious leader who persecuted and helped murder Christians and made their lives miserable by throwing them in jail for preaching about Jesus. Here is where it gets interesting. In Acts chapter 9, Paul (named Saul at that time) had an encounter with Jesus on the road to Damascus. This is the very trip on which he took letters from the high priest to arrest Christians for their faith in the Way, Jesus Christ.

Saul's Conversion

Meanwhile, Saul was still breathing out murderous threats against the Lord's disciples. He went to the high priest and asked him for letters to the synagogues in Damascus, so that if he found any there who belonged to the Way, whether men or women, he might take them as prisoners to Jerusalem. As he neared Damascus on his journey, suddenly a light from heaven flashed around him. He fell to the ground and heard a voice say to him, "Saul, Saul, why do you persecute me?" "Who are you, Lord?" Saul asked. "I am Jesus, whom you are persecuting," he replied. "Now get up and go into the city, and you will be told what you must do." (Acts 9:1–6)

Oh, how I would love to have witnessed this encounter! As mentioned earlier, Saul was affiliated with the religious leaders of his day who tried to stop the Christian movement. The disciples and Christians considered him a thorn in their side, a messenger from Satan. But wouldn't you know that God had other plans for Saul because after his encounter with the Creator, he was never the same? God had plans for him that put that man on warp speed to spread the gospel to the world.

Here is my favorite part of Paul's conversation during his Damascus Road encounter with Jesus. I hope you're getting excited. This is going to be good! There is so much revelation in this encounter, I could burst with excitement! Remember my paraphrase of God's response to Paul? Keep that in mind when you read this next part. God showed me something so awesome!

The men traveling with Saul stood there speechless; they heard the sound but did not see anyone. Saul got up from the ground, but when he opened his eyes he could see nothing. So they led him by the hand into Damascus. For three days, he was blind, and did not eat or drink anything. In Damascus, there was a disciple named Ananias. The Lord called to him in a vision, "Ananias!" "Yes, Lord," he answered. The Lord told him, "Go to the house of Judas on *Straight Street* and ask for a man from Tarsus named Saul, for he is praying. In a vision, he has seen a man named Ananias come and place his hands on him to restore his sight." "Lord," Ananias answered, "I have heard many reports about this man and all the harm he has done to your holy people in Jerusalem. And he has come here with authority from the chief priests to arrest all who call on your name." But the Lord said to Ananias, "Go! This man is my chosen instrument to proclaim my name to the Gentiles and their kings and to the people of Israel. I will show him how much he must suffer for my name." (Acts 9:7–15 emphasis added)

Did you get it? I want you to notice a few key words in these Scriptures that literally got my hands raised and mouth shouting for joy in the excitement of this revelation. I love how Saul was sitting blinded by the power of God in a house on *Straight Street*. I am sure the disciples who were afraid of Saul had to be praying that he would have a miraculous encounter with Jesus Christ. Saul was a hindrance to the body of Christ, and God just set that man straight! Do you see the correlation of the street and the prayers of the saints for Paul? Even with all the persecution and murdering of the Christians in which Saul participated, God had mercy on him when he surrendered his life to Jesus. The Lord sent Ananias as a messenger of hope, not a messenger of torment to Saul. This encounter not only changed his life but the continued path that he was on. This conversion removed the roadblock that allowed the message of Christ to spread throughout the earth to this present day.

Then Ananias went to the house and entered it. Placing his hands on Saul, he said, "Brother Saul, the Lord—Jesus, who appeared to you on the road as you were coming here—has sent me so that you may see again and be filled with the Holy Spirit." Immediately, something like scales fell from Saul's eyes, and he could see again. He got up and was baptized, and after taking some food, he regained his strength. (Acts 9:17–19)

Do you realize that Paul wrote twelve or thirteen books of the New Testament? God had huge plans for him. Why do you think Satan kept tormenting him? Why do you think Satan torments the body of Christ as he does even in our churches today? Satan wants to use every weapon he can to stop the move of the Holy Spirit and transform lives with the Word of God. He will use people as thorns to stop us! The marvelous news is that we can halt his mission against us with the authority over the enemy through the name of Jesus.

This is the point I want to drive home to you. Before our transformation with Christ, we all did things of which we are not proud. Now that we are Christ-followers, we know that God requires us to live a holy life. Sometimes it is a long process for people to change their old behaviors but for some it is a radical transformation, and their walk with God is at warp speed. Paul faced many challenges with his fellow brothers and sisters in the Christian church. I strongly urge you to take the time to study Paul's letters to the Corinthians. One of the best translations I read to help me fully understand his letters was in *The Message* Bible.

I have encountered several thorns in my side during my walk with the Lord, especially since I fully surrendered my life to Christ. And I must tell you that the closer you get to God, the more the enemy isn't going to like it. Satan will try to use whoever and whatever he can to try and stop the message of Jesus from going out from you. But don't let this stop you. You have come this far, and it's time to push on through for what you have been praying for. If anything, it should get you fired up to know that God has a great plan and purpose for your life and the lives of those whom God brings to you. It's just like having a baby. The intensity becomes more challenging and painful just before the baby is born. That mom isn't smiling when she is birthing that baby. She is laser-focused, and she knows she has a job to do to birth that baby who is the reward for all her suffering. In the end, she has a great gift in her hands and a job well done from all those in the labor room cheering her on.

I don't want to give all Paul's thorns away in this writing because he faced some pretty wild things on his journey to preach the gospel. I want you to go and study Paul's journey for yourself. I think you will find it interesting that you have encountered many of the same issues or obstacles when you read his letters to the churches he mentored.

Oh, and don't be surprised when someone comes from your past to try and remind you of how offensive you once were. Then on the flip side of the coin, don't be upset when you are frustrated like Paul with people who are trying to stop the flow of the gospel and the calling God has on your life. God's grace is sufficient for you to get through these obstacles. You are here on this earth on an assignment to reach the people to whom God has called you. As challenging as they can be, these people are in your sphere of influence for a reason. When you are frustrated with them, reflect on how God was patient with you and set you straight to the Way who is Jesus, our Lord and Savior. I like what my friend Martha Bootle says, "We need God's grace the most when we are learning to walk in love with other people."

God did some amazing things in Paul's life. He experienced signs and wonders he could brag about all day long to others, but it's not Paul who should receive the glory. God gets the glory. God is an amazing God. Honestly, I don't know how people live without Him. I love when the Holy Spirit gives me fresh revelation on a subject I am curious to learn more about. Even if someone doesn't agree with me, that's all right. Just

PAPA GOD AND ASHLEY

like Paul, I will not focus on the hardships or the opinions of others. I will focus and appreciate the gifts God is showing me, and I will keep pressing on to the mark. I will run my race and finish it even if you don't agree with me because I have my race, and you have yours. It's how we finish the race that matters to God.

This is the best news of all. If you seek God in all matters, He will give you the strength to overcome any thorn that tries to dig into you through the power and wisdom of the Holy Spirit. Without Jesus, we can do nothing, but with Him, all things are possible for those who believe. God will set those people who are thorns in your side, straight. All God requires of you and me is to pray for them and believe that He has great plans for those people, and so you must stay in His grace. If we do our part, then God can do His part.

God removes the thorns eventually. It may not be in the way we would like, but He will do it in a way that is pleasing to Him and helps others. His plans and timing are strategic. That doesn't mean people have the right to abuse you. But let God use you in a healthy manner and in the way He needs to. He is your strength, and that strength will carry you through.

Big hugs,
Papa God and Ashley

The Anchor for Our Souls

My family lives not too far from the bay, and we love to go boating in the summer. We see all kinds of sea life and go island hopping to look for sea shells. I love the ocean because it reminds me of how small we really are in this big and amazing world. God loves us so much that this world was created by Him just for us to explore.

When we island hop, we must get our boat close enough to the island and then drop our anchor so that our boat doesn't drift away with the changing tide and crashing waves. Once we know the boat is secure, we can grab our towels, jump into the water about knee deep, and head for land to soak up the sun and just relax. But if we are careless and our anchor is not fixed into the ocean floor, we could find ourselves taking a long swim in the ocean or, perhaps, stranded. If we are not paying close attention to a change in weather, there is a high probability that our boat could be destroyed if the winds get too strong.

The safety of our vessel and that anchor reminds me of why it is so important to have a strong tie spiritually with God through Jesus Christ. "We have this hope as an anchor for the soul, firm and secure. It enters the inner sanctuary behind the curtain, where our forerunner, Jesus, has entered on our behalf. He has become a high priest forever, in the order of Melchizedek" (Heb. 6:19–20).

Since I am a visual person, I'll say it like this: When a military boat puts its massive anchor into the ocean, that boat isn't moving; that anchor weighs tons and is very strong. The storm winds may come, and the waves will crash and roar their ugly heads, but that boat is steadfast in that spot; it isn't going anywhere.

The Bible says that Jesus is an anchor to my soul meaning our emotions, feelings, and thoughts. This anchor reaches into the throne room of heaven behind the veil where God sits. Romans 8:34 says that Jesus has already gone ahead of us and is seated at the right hand of the Father interceding for us on our behalf.

Wow! That is so awesome! You are chosen to be His, and His promises are forever. God never changes, and He is not shaken by what shakes us. Hebrews 13:8 says that Jesus Christ is the same yesterday, today, and forever.

When fear, hopelessness, and doubt try to creep in your mind, remember His promises to us as believers. Our hope is not in the things of this world. It is in the unmovable, unshakable God who is in you and me.

With God on our side, it doesn't matter what someone else says about us or tries to do to us. We serve an immovable God. Once we know who we are in Christ, we are immovable by our circumstances as well. I understand that it's not easy to remain at peace about a situation; it takes spiritual maturity to act like Christ. "Until we all reach unity in the faith and in the knowledge of the Son of God and become mature, attaining to the whole measure of the fullness of Christ. Then we will no longer be infants, tossing back and forth by the waves, and blown by the cunning and craftiness of people in their deceitful scheming" (Eph. 4:13–14).

Give your problems to God and have hope in Him that He will hold you steady through the storms of life. Drop your anchor in the presence of the Holy of Holies. He's got you. Pick up your sword (the Bible) and use His name. *Jesus!*

Be confident in the Lord and praise Him. Start declaring the promises of God over your life and say, "Because of You, Lord, my boat isn't moving! You, Lord, are holding me steadfast to Your promises."

Now read Hebrews 6:19–20 out loud, slap Satan around with it a few times, and say, "Jesus is my hope, and He has my back, so I will not be moved by how I feel!" Remind Satan that he lost his authority a long time ago, so he needs to get lost, in the name of Jesus. "Take that, devil." Ha! Ha! Ha!

Through the blood of Jesus, you have the inheritance of victory, peace, and joy. And know this: You *will* overcome through the blood of Jesus, and the word of your testimony will set you and others free in Christ Jesus. "So, if the Son sets you free, you will be free indeed" (John 8:36).

If you keep declaring these Scriptures, I promise you the storms will cease once you get this deeply rooted in your soul. You will become unmovable no matter what the enemy tries to throw at you. And when you pray, pray with authority over the enemy. Make it your mission that when you walk into a room, all the demons shake and run for their lives to just get away from you. That's an awesome revelation, isn't it? Now, just laugh at the devil with great joy because Jesus lives inside of you. Ha! Ha! Ha!

You believe that there is one God. Good! Even the demons believe that—and shudder. (James 2:19)

Submit yourselves, then, to God. Resist the devil, and he will flee from you. (James 4:7)

Jesus in you is the reason they must flee and even shake when you walk in the authority He gave you. Keep on praising the Lord with all that is in you because He has already won this battle. That's because your thoughts and emotions are unmovable; your anchor is secured in the throne room of heaven. Amen!

Big hugs,
Papa God and Ashley

Your Weaknesses Are Your Strengths

When I was a little girl, my parents would have me quote Scriptures like Philippians 4:13 KJV which says, "I can do all things through Christ who strengthens me" and Romans 8:37, "No, in all these things we are more than conquerors through him who loves us." Of course, I would shorten them to make the Scripture more personal and say, "I am more than a conqueror, and I can do anything I set my mind to because Christ lives in me." My parents would have me repeat these verses daily until I had not only memorized them, but I believed them, too. Once I believed them, I started acting differently. I had more confidence in myself because I knew what God said about me.

I struggled in school during my youth. It's not that I wasn't capable; it's that as a little girl, I did not have the desire to dedicate myself to studying. My mind was not yet trained to pay close attention to what my teachers were saying and understand that what they taught was important for the tests and quizzes. After failing several tests, I started to think I was not smart enough, so I would give up instead of focusing and working harder. This was a tactic of the enemy to try and stop me from what God had purposed for me, but God had better plans!

As a child, I was inquisitive and I loved to talk. My teachers would tell my parents that I made friends with everyone I sat next to in my class. It did not matter who; I always encouraged others to converse with me. I also had this amazing gift to change any subject to the topic of my choice. Well, some things never change because I still have the gift of gab and the ability to persuade!

At that time, however, it may have been frustrating for my parents and my teachers to keep me focused on school, but God had a plan from the start for His purpose in my life. I truly love people, and I love to find out more about them. I have never met a stranger, especially one that wants to engage in a good conversation. It's funny how God instills these gifts in us when we are very young, since as an adult, speaking and writing are the biggest part of my career.

Like everyone, I have strengths and weaknesses. As I have grown in life and in the Lord, I have come to realize that the weaknesses I thought I had are now my strengths. My parents were very smart to get my mind on what Christ says about me and what He could do in and through me. The focus was to use my strengths and get my mind off my own self-condemnation. The apostle Paul says it like this: "That is why, for Christ's sake, I delight in weaknesses, in insults, in hardships, in persecutions, in difficulties. For when I am weak, then I am strong" (2 Cor. 12:10).

I have learned to focus and conquer my weaknesses through meditating on God's Word. I have also brought this same pattern of thinking into my own children's lives. As an example, every day on the way to drop my daughter off at school, we speak out Scripture and speak life into our day. It is something I learned from my own mom, and now I have passed this down to my children. I have noticed that her confidence has skyrocketed over the past few years since we have been doing this. She can even finish the Scriptures before I am finished saying them, and I love that!

Like me, her grades went from one of the lowest in the class to high honor roll all year long. Praise God! The Word of God is wisdom and revelation knowledge. It breaks every curse, every chain, and sets our lives on a course of victory in Christ Jesus!

I encourage you to focus on the strengths you have been given as a gift from God. When you do this, use those gifts to glorify the Lord through you. Don't let the enemy deceive you that you are not good enough or smart enough. That kind of thinking will only allow him to get you off track and keep you frozen in fear.

After all, you were made in the image of our Creator. He created you for such a time as this with a very important task on this earth for the kingdom of God.

Start speaking life into your day and with others around you. Scripture says in Proverbs 18:21 that life and death are in the power of your tongue, meaning you will become what you say and believe about yourself. If you change what you say about yourself, you will notice that your day will turn around, and that will affect the outcome of your purpose and the purpose of others. God has called each of us to do something unique on this earth for His kingdom.

If you don't know what that purpose is yet, talk to God and ask Him to show you. He will tell you through that still, small voice and through His written Word.

Here are a few other Scriptures you can use to declare the promises of God over yourself and your children. Make sure you personalize them, and please find other Scriptures you can relate to on your own as well. When you read these Scriptures, personalize them by replacing the word *you* with the words *I* or *me*.

You, dear children, are from God and have overcome them, because the one who is in you is greater than the one who is in the world. (1 John 4:4)

Personalized: Because I am a child of God, I have overcome anything that is contrary to what God says about me. Greater is He (God) who is in me than he (Satan) who is in this world.

Now try this same concept in the next few Scriptures.

If God is for us, who can be against us? (Rom. 8:31)

Personalized: If God is for *me,* who can be against *me?*

Now you personalize these next Scriptures and rewrite them below:

The LORD himself goes before you and will be with you; he will never leave you nor forsake you. Do not be afraid; do not be discouraged. (Deut. 31:8)

Personalize and rewrite the Scripture: _____
_____
_____
_____
_____

Do Not Worry

Therefore, I tell you, do not worry about your life, what you will eat or drink; or about your body, what you will wear. Is not life more than food, and the body more than clothes? (Matt. 6:25)

Personalize and rewrite the Scripture: _____
_____
_____
_____
_____

I pray that God strengthens you through these declarations, and that you fulfill all that He has for you. Get these Scriptures so deeply rooted in your soul that nothing can move you from the truth. Don't give up when you feel like you're failing. You may at times be weak, but you are not a failure. You were never created to fail. You were created to connect with your Papa God to let Him show you how to use those weaknesses as lessons to turn them into strengths. Those strengths are already in you.

Be strong and courageous because you *can* do *all* things through Christ who gives you strength.

Big hugs,
Papa God and Ashley

No Trespassing on Holy Ground

I have always wanted to visit Jerusalem and see the temple where Jesus stood. Since there currently is no temple in Jerusalem, we can only imagine what it looked like. In 1 Kings 6–8 we read that King Solomon, the son of King David, built the temple for God. These Scriptures give a great description of how it was built, the dimensions, and the objects placed there.

Since I am a visual person, I looked up pictures on the Internet to see what it may have looked like versus my imagination from the Bible's descriptions. (See 1 Kings 6, 2 Chronicles 3.) It was magnificent! Just realizing all the detail King Solomon put into it was breathtaking. He built it with the best materials the earth has in its wealth of treasures. Before Solomon built this temple, I am sure he was thinking he would build only the best for his Creator.

I could see all the stone, gold, bronze, and wood that made up the structure of the building. Solomon even had artwork designed for the inside and outside of the temple including flowers, palm trees, cherubim, bulls, and lions that stood at full attention.

What must the people have thought as they walked into the temple? The looks on their faces must have been priceless; I am sure it was a grand sight to see. I can imagine that everyone was in great amazement in regard to the structure's beauty. This was no ordinary temple!

Solomon did all of this out of obedience to God and his father, King David, before him just to have a house for the Ark of the Covenant. This is where God would reside so they could come to worship Him and make atoning sacrifices to Him for the forgiveness of the sins of His people.

As I was reading about the temple, the Lord brought to my attention how He no longer lives in the Ark of the Covenant. When Jesus died, the Holy Spirit came out of that temple, and now we are the temple of the Holy Spirit; we are a temple not made by human hands but a place where God resides in every believer.

So in the eyes of God, we, too, are no ordinary temple. This is so important for us to understand. With that thought in mind, think about how special your body is to God. Just for you and me, Jesus came to earth in human form and paid a high price with His life just so the Holy Spirit could enter our bodies, His new temple. "With a loud cry, Jesus breathed his last. The curtain of the temple was torn in two from top to bottom. And when the centurion, who stood there in front of Jesus, saw how he died, he said, 'Surely this man was the Son of God!'" (Mark 15:37–39).

Praise God! When Jesus took His last breath on the cross, the Spirit of God came out of the Ark of the Covenant sitting in the temple in Jerusalem. The curtain that separated us from the Holy of Holies tore in two, releasing the curse that had been upon humanity by the sins of Adam.

Can you imagine seeing in the spirit realm when the veil was torn and God came out of the Ark of the Covenant? Jesus died and rose again to live in us! We are the house of God!

When I read Mark 15:37–39 for the first time, it was an aha moment, and I hope you are seeing this verse with the same lenses. God no longer lives in the Ark of the Covenant; He came out when the veil was torn and now lives in the believer. The veil hung in the temple separating the Holy of Holies, and only a high priest could enter once a year. The veil torn in the temple represents the veil over our eyes (deception due to sin), which was torn when we believed that Jesus is the Son of God and accepted Him as our Lord and Savior.

The Lord reminded me that we, our bodies, are so much more valuable than a physical structure. Satan has no right to attack the temple of God. If he does, he is trespassing. In addition to that, we have no right to clutter up our temples with a bunch of junk. Our bodies are considered holy ground. That goes for what we listen to, watch, and put on or in our bodies. Wow! That's tough talk, right? Sorry, don't shoot the messenger. "Do you not know that your bodies are temples of the Holy Spirit, who is in you, whom you have received from God? You are not your own; you were bought at a price. Therefore, honor God with your bodies" (1 Cor. 6:19–20).

I also noticed in the picture of the temple that there were lookout points on each corner and on the tower for the soldiers to keep watch for any invaders. The enemy is always trying to invade our minds and cause us to stumble or fall. We must be very protective of our thoughts and actions. I have learned that if something comes on the television or radio and I know it's not good for me to see or hear, I change the channel or turn it off. I don't want those images or thoughts in my head.

If we make a mistake, thank God there is forgiveness of sins, for we all sin. But when we stumble, we must get back up and remember who we are in Christ. We need to stand on guard and not allow the enemy to invade our territory. When we repent, confess our sins, and ask for forgiveness, we do an about face. True repentance is a turning around in the opposite direction of the where you previously faced. Think about it like this: If you are looking south, then when you turn around in the opposite direction, you are now looking north.

Our bodies have built-in lookouts called senses: sight, hearing, touch, smell, taste, and the sixth sense, our spiritual sense. When we do something we know is wrong, our spiritual alarm will go off saying, "No, don't do that" or "Get as far away as possible because this is dangerous to the temple!"

I am sure they had trumpets to sound alarms in the temple. We have a built-in alarm/trumpet. It's called a mouth. When you start to feel attacks coming, sound the alarm and tell the enemy to get lost and go away from your temple in the name of Jesus.

Because God is living in your temple, you are to protect it always. Grab your sword, which is your Bible, stand your ground, and fight against the enemy when he tries to attack your temple. "Submit yourselves, then, to God. Resist the devil, and he will flee from you" (James 4:7). Remember who you are today and who lives in you. Don't allow the enemy a chance sneak into the Holy of Holies. He's not welcomed or allowed to step his skanky foot on holy ground. Our Papa God lives in there!

Big hugs,
Papa God and Ashley

Concrete Heart

Have you ever met anyone who was calloused at heart? You may be thinking there is nothing you could say or do to soften their feelings toward you or toward a situation. At times, it appears their hearts are made of concrete. They are so hardened that it seems they are not happy about anything. Everything that comes out of their mouths is nasty and sounds like the devil himself. In instances like this, I always wonder what happened in their lives to cause such personal torment leading to their concrete heart.

The Lord said something to my spirit about people like this. He said, "People who need to be loved the most seem to be the ones who deserve it the least. But I AM love, and if I live in you, then My love is already in you. Through you, I will show them My love because I love them." God may not like what that person is saying or doing, but He still loves them, and He wants them to be saved and come into a relationship with Him.

I think it is a normal reaction for our flesh to want to turn away from people who have wronged us or who are always difficult to be around. But these people need to know they are loved more than anyone else!

Something has happened in their lives causing them to shut down their feelings and push others out. Hurt and anger will try to pass on to you, but don't let it! The buck stops with you!

We have a choice how to react to this situation. Do we fight back with hate, or do we fight back with love? Scripture says in 1 Corinthians 13:8 that "Love never fails." Love continues even when someone is rude and nasty to us. God's love keeps no record of past wrongs. For true healing to take place in that person, we must listen to the voice of truth, which is the voice of God. "For this people's heart has become calloused; they hardly hear with their ears, and they have closed their eyes. Otherwise, they might see with their eyes, hear with their ears, understand with their hearts and turn, and I would heal them. But blessed are your eyes because they see, and your ears because they hear" (Matt. 13:15–16).

The person who cannot seek God has their hearts so hardened by the burdens of life that they shut down everything and everyone to try to protect themselves. They have built up walls so no one can hurt them, but what they don't realize is the One who can heal them and make them whole is ready and willing to send someone like you to help draw them closer to God. Only through the spoken Word of God can those concrete walls fall so that He can mend their broken and hardened hearts.

If you are thinking of someone right now and God is saying to you, "Through you I will show them My love because I love them," take on that challenge. It may not be the easiest task set before you, but God will reward you for your obedience. He has opened your eyes to this person for a reason, for His purpose. Satan always attacks the ones who have the most purpose for the kingdom of God. Everyone needs to know that they are loved by their Creator. For those who are lost, it might well be someone like you who can see them the way God sees them.

Keep in mind, it is not your job to fix that person, and you should never be someone's doormat. If the relationship is abusive physically or emotionally, you need to distance yourself. God does not tolerate abuse. You must set boundaries in dealing with people in a difficult situation.

However, it's your job as a believer to stand in the gap in prayer for that person out of a pure and genuine heart. I have learned to forgive often and pray more.

One of my favorite Scriptures to stand in the gap for someone I love is Ezekiel 36:26. "I will give you a new heart and put a new spirit in you; I will remove from you your heart of stone and give you a heart of flesh" (Ezek. 36:26).

When I have prayed this over a person, I put their name in the verse where it says the word *you* and replace word *I* with God. I will say something like this, "God, give _____ (fill a name in the blank) a new heart and put a new spirit in _____; remove from them a heart of stone and give _____ a heart of flesh." Every situation is different, but I am confident that someone at one point in your life took the time to pray for you and was patient with you. They loved you through a time when maybe your heart was like concrete.

I want to encourage you to soften your heart to the person God has brought to your mind. It's now your turn to spread the love of God and be the light in a dark and lonely world. Release your prayers to Him and then watch what He does to that person's heart. The walls of concrete will start to chip away and break down. The reason is because love conquers all. It's the greatest force in the universe. God designed it that way because God *is* love. "And now these three remain faith, hope and love. But the greatest of these is love" (1 Cor. 13:13).

Stay strong in the Word and keep on loving them like Jesus did. Use the authority He gave us with the name of Jesus. Keep yourself built up in prayer and seek the Lord's guidance always. Some hardened hearts take a little longer because the wound is so deep and the enemy's hold on them is strong. But the power of God's love is stronger. My experience with this is that if your love and prayers for them are consistent, the breakthrough is on its way.

Big hugs,
Papa God and Ashley

Center Stage

The Lord gave me a vision. In this vision, the room is filled with voices of multitudes of people with enthusiasm. Lights are flashing all around what looks like to be an arena with beams of lights going every which way. Then the room goes dark as a spotlight hits the center stage. Every eye is drawn to the stage just waiting to see who will be standing in the middle of the room. You can hear the crowd go silent and all movement stops because as they look out, there is no one standing on the stage.

During this vision, I could feel hearts sinking in their chests while saying, "What is going on? Have our expectations not been met? We have been waiting, and there's nothing here to be seen."

Some say, "No! It cannot be. There has to be something more."

All of a sudden, a small voice from the crowd speaks up and starts chanting that name above all names. It's that wonderful and powerful name. "Jesus! Jesus! Jesus! Jesus! This is who we are waiting for," they say.

Others agree and join in the chant in unison saying, "Jesus! Jesus! Jesus! Jesus!"

The arena lights go dark again and the room goes black for a few seconds. The sounds of thunder start to gargle and lightning strikes with a bright flash, lighting up the sky above.

They can now see the sky is beautifully adorned in brilliant colors, even colors they have never seen before. The winds suddenly start to whistle and howl. Everyone starts to look all around and at each other. Through their whispers, they start to ask, "What is happening?"

Then it happens! Jesus appears in the center of the stage, lighting up the room like a bright star. All eyes try to refocus and adjust to the light change. Then those who can see more clearly gaze in on Him. Many fall down on their faces, while the rest of the crowd erupts in a wild cheer of anticipation for this is the moment they have all been waiting for.

Suddenly, the Holy Spirit joins the show with a mighty wind at His heels, and the peace and love of God sweeps through the crowd. They can all feel Him with every fiber of their being. The breath of God covers them. It flows over their bodies, in and throughout them.

The time is at hand, and everyone knows it. These are the ones who had been waiting for so long; they knew this day would eventually come. They had read and heard about it from their pastors, members of their churches, and their loved ones.

As they look around them, they can see others they knew on earth and some they only heard of in Scripture, but somehow, they knew them by name. They look at each other with a big smile in amazement. The moment seems surreal as they watch on.

I can only imagine the thoughts that ran through their minds. They thank God that they had lived by faith and not by sight in what seemed to be their natural realm in the years before. But this is a distant memory for them now, and something new is about to begin.

Before this moment, some did not believe, and so they did not see. Woe to them who chose not to see because they did not want to see and chose not to hear the Word of the Lord. The believers are the selected ones, and so they do see.

They saw their Lord and Savior face to face standing before them. All the battles have been waged and won. They cry out, "Holy, holy, holy is the Lamb."

Rejoicing and singing with all hands raised and hearts abandoned, nothing or no one else matters. The past is behind them, and they can't help to think that it was all worth it for this moment.

The angels start to sing, "Glory to Him who sits on the throne of heaven and earth, Jesus in the highest. The Light of the World has come!"

Instruments join in with the singing, and everyone knows the words so they, too, start to sing the praises of their Lord and Savior. The sound is beautiful and breathtaking all at the same time. Hearts rejoice with gladness for the One who has taken center stage. The great celebration has begun. "Rejoice, rejoice, rejoice," they say. There is no more sorrow and no more tears. The Light of the World is here."

The Day of the Lord

Now, brothers and sisters, about times and dates we do not need to write to you, for you know very well that the day of the Lord will come like a thief in the night. While people are saying, "Peace and safety," destruction will come on them suddenly, as labor pains on a pregnant woman, and they will not escape. But you, brothers and sisters, are not in darkness so that this day should surprise you like a thief. You are all children of the light and children of the day. We do not belong to the night or to the darkness. So then, let us not be like others, who are asleep, but let us be awake and sober. For those who sleep, sleep at night, and those who get drunk, get drunk at night. But since we belong to the day, let us be sober, putting on faith and love as a breastplate, and the hope of salvation as a helmet. For God did not appoint us to suffer wrath but to receive salvation through our Lord Jesus Christ. He died for us so that, whether we are awake or asleep, we may live together with him. Therefore, encourage one another and build each other up, just as in fact you are doing. (1 Thess. 5:1–11)

My dear friend, are you ready? Do your eyes see the coming of our Lord and Savior? It's not a matter of if He is coming. It is written in the Word of God that He will come. The prophecies foretold of this day long ago so that no one would have an excuse for missing the return of Jesus Christ. Yes, all prophecy must come to pass before this great and glorious day. Are you watching and listening as these prophecies are being fulfilled? It seems that every day that passes, prophecy is being fulfilled by the numbers. Prophecies in books like Ezekiel, Daniel, and Revelation are coming to pass in our local news. Time is drawing near to that glorious day.

Those who are awake will know when the time is near. I am watching, and I can see that the time is close. Get ready because soon Jesus will take center stage. Before He does, there is still a little time left because there is much to do before His coming. We must wake up the sleepers. There are many rooms still left to be filled in heaven. "Do not let your hearts be troubled. You believe in God; believe also in me. My Father's house has many rooms; if that were not so, would I have told you that I am going there to prepare a place for you? And if I go and prepare a place for you, I will come back and take you to be with me that you also may be where I am" (John 14:1–3).

We are all invited to the celebration, but it is up to you and me whether to attend or not. If you are like me, this is exciting news, and I can't wait to see Jesus standing before me. I choose Jesus, I choose to be there in His presence, and I choose to live each day as if it were my last.

My heart longs for that glorious day to be in the presence of my Papa God. Oh God, let your people awaken! The time of slumber is no more for I feel that the celebration is near. I hear the voice of the Lord say, "Come all. I will be waiting for you center stage. Have you called out My name? The time is now to choose." "For many are invited, but few are chosen" (Matt. 22:14).

For the person reading this, I hope this vision gives you great joy because of the return of our Lord, but I know there are many who are not prepared. There is a reason why you are reading this book; God wants you and others around you to be ready to enter into His glory. If you have loved ones and friends who are not ready for the return of Christ, start declaring that their eyes are opened and that their hearts are tender to hear the voice of God speaking to them. Pray for their salvation so that one day when we are standing there looking at Jesus, others who walked this life with us will be standing there, too. No matter what you think or see, God wants all to be there on the day our Messiah returns.

Declaration: I declare over _____ (fill name or names in the blank) that their eyes will be opened to the truth, and that their hearts will receive Jesus as their Lord and Savior. Holy Spirit, come over my family and loved ones like a mighty wind and breathe Your life into their spirit, soul, and body. I declare that they come out of their slumber and are alive in Christ Jesus. Fill them up with Your love, Lord. Your kingdom come and Your will be done on earth as it is in heaven. In Jesus' name, amen.

Big hugs,
Papa God and Ashley

Running the Race

The apostle Paul wrote about running the race God has set before us. What race is he talking about? I run around all day going here and there trying to get things done on my list. Whether it be running around for work, my family, or visiting with friends, I typically have my schedule planned weeks ahead of time.

In 1 Corinthians 9:24–25, Paul is talking about having the self-discipline to run the race of life for God. He has plans for our lives with the end goal of our life in full view. This plan for us is our course or journey that leads to the victory prize in Christ Jesus.

The Need for Self-Discipline

Do you not know that in a race all the runners run, but only one gets the prize? Run in such a way as to get the prize. Everyone who competes in the games goes into strict training. They do it to get a crown that will not last, but we do it to get a crown that will last forever. (1 Cor. 9:24–25)

I have heard that professional athletes train anywhere from twelve to twenty hours a week for about eight years to be the best at their sport. Their goal is to compete with other athletes on an Olympic level. The athletes have a goal set before them, their plan is to win the race, not just participate with the others in order to be seen on the track. No, he or she is on a mission to be the champion and to win the title as the best in that field! Their goal is to come home with gold medals.

Let's dig deeper into this conversation because chances are you are not an Olympic athlete, nor am I. However, in this race called life, our goal is to condition our minds to think like one. It doesn't matter if you're a runner, a manager, or a sales representative for a corporation. Whatever job you do for a living, everyone competes in some fashion in their lives to be the best at what they do. It's as if a strong desire to win is naturally instilled in us as children. I think we all can agree that it is more fun to win than it is to lose at anything. We all want to be in first place because then there is recognition and praise, and it feels great to be noticed and rewarded as the best!

Have you ever seen siblings competing for the best toy or to get their parents' attention? I even see it in my pets when I come home. The little one gets all excited and jumps up and down trying to be the first to get my attention. The bigger one just pushes her way through to see me, and since she is over a hundred pounds, she usually makes me stop before I can move past her. They typically will not stop until I have said hello with a sweet voice and make direct eye contact with them, telling them how happy I am to see them, too. I love their unconditional love.

There are people who may not be as competitive, but I guarantee you they still want to feel they are important and noticed by others. God created us all to have different personalities, but the goal is for us to be loved and appreciated. Did you know that God's most valuable possession is people? The sad part is that there are many who don't know their value and worth. "Blessed are those who find wisdom, those who gain understanding, for she is more profitable than silver and yields better returns than gold. She is more precious than rubies; nothing you desire can compare with her. Long life is in her right hand; in her left hand are riches and honor" (Prov. 3:13–16).

Most of the time, these people find themselves feeling empty because they are looking for love and their self-worth from others. So where is the prize in all of this since we all stumble at some point in our lives? When our own selfishness wants to be first, it seems that someone must be in second place. When Jesus was about to go on the cross, He told His disciples that the last will be first and the first will be last. (See Matt. 20:16.) Are we so vain that we put ourselves and our own selfish motives above what God has planned for us, so that we lose the real focus of our purpose on this earth?

I know for me, distractions can come very easily, especially when I feel frustrated and over-tired. When this happens, I know it is time to refocus and examine myself. It's time to start thinking about where and what I am spending my time chasing after. I don't want to run a race with my hands flying aimlessly around in the air and saying, "Pick me, choose me, and see me."

To finish this race the way God intends, we first must put His will into our lives. Even if it means taking second place or last place and pushing someone else on ahead of us for the win. Our worth is not in people; our worth is found in Jesus. People will fail us because they are human, but God never will, and His love is everlasting.

My friend, God does see us, and He chooses you and me. God has a divine plan for each of His children. Just because we are running as fast as we can doesn't mean we are winning or that we are even heading the right direction to the finish line.

Once this has become a revelation, you may need to ask yourself, "In what race am I running? What has held my attention so tightly that I can't stop and spend time with God and seek Him for the answers?"

I mean, really, why do we do this to ourselves? I understand; I've done it, too. But when I stop and think about it all, it just seems so senseless in the whole scheme of life.

It seems that we can get caught up in the things of this world that misdirect us to a dead-end prize. Since the things of this world will wear out or give way, our goal should be to chase after the desires God has in store for us, not chasing objects or people. After all, it works out better for us in the end anyway when we chase after what God wants for us. "Therefore, I do not run like someone running aimlessly; I do not fight like a boxer beating the air. No, I strike a blow to my body and make it my slave so that after I have preached to others, I myself will not be disqualified for the prize" (1 Cor. 9:26–27).

The Holy Spirit is an amazing coach. God has not left you alone to figure out how to run the race without instruction and encouragement. He has already given you what you need to win the race through His written Word. The Word of God is a love letter to us with instructions as our manual to life. The Bible is our manual for victory!

Our special gifts or talents are gifts for His glory and purpose to be fulfilled in our lives on this earth. Think about the story of the tortoise and the hare. The hare was fast, so he seemed like the top dog in the race, while the tortoise had the disadvantage; he moved very slowly. But the hare got arrogant and ran as fast as he could but then decided to waste his time and take a nap on the sidelines. The tortoise slowly kept moving ahead with the end of the race in mind. Then the hare woke up and sped on ahead, but he got distracted again by the pretty ladies and started showing off his talents to them. Meanwhile, the tortoise kept slowly moving ahead and passed the hare. Suddenly, the hare heard cheering from the crowd, but it was too late; he lost the race, and the underdog won in the end.

So my question to you is this: Which race are you running? If your race looks like the hare's race, and you have all these wonderful

God-given talents, don't think for a second that Satan isn't just waiting to lure you to sleep or distract you with someone good looking so that you miss crossing that finish line in victory. You were on assignment from the moment you took your first breath to the moment you take your last breath. Satan hates your guts, and he has an assignment, too. His assignment is to take you out and distract you from your race.

If you're like the tortoise, you might be slow at getting to where you plan to go but you are determined to get there. Along the way there are others who may be asleep and distracted. *Wake them up!* Tell them it's time to keep moving.

It's OK to slow down and ask God what to do next. It's not OK to think we have this race in the bag because our talents are stronger or better than someone else's. We can't become complacent with the gifts and talents God gave us, and we certainly can't be held down by dead weights that prevent us from moving forward.

After much prayer on a subject, one of my favorite questions to ask Papa God is, "What do You say about that, Papa?" Then I ask Him, "Where do we go next?" Then I am silent and wait to hear that still, small voice. Don't try to overthink it. His answer will be clear if you wait in silence and truly seek His will. To be honest, there are times that the answers will not come right away. At times, I've had to wait patiently and fine-tune my spiritual ears to hear God's reply. But if we keep seeking Him, the answers always come.

The ultimate prize in this race of life is getting to know Him and learning who you are in Christ and what you are to accomplish next through Him. Being a Christian isn't just about making it to heaven. It's about the choices we make with the opportunities God gives us while we are living life here on earth.

Once you know your purpose, He will show you where to go and how to get there. I can tell you that the more that I get to know God, the more I realize that His purpose is love, and that means His people are to share His love and compassion with others as well. Remember, God holds value in people, not just Christians, but all people. John 3:16 ESV says, "For so God loved the world [people] that He gave His only Son." God wants us to give others what He gave to us. To do that, we must engage with God and others to do what He did for people.

So however God plays that out for you, go after that goal with the crown of victory set before you. Be the person God has called you to be without hesitation. My mentor, Pastor Debra Kaplan, always tells me, "Ashley, just do it afraid if you have to."

My friend, you must take the first step to get started. God loves you and will be there for you when you do. Don't be afraid to step out in faith. Be afraid *not* to step out into your calling and purpose because that is where the victories are waiting for you at the finish line. "Do not store up for yourselves treasures on earth, where moths and vermin destroy, and where thieves break in and steal. But store up for yourselves treasures in heaven, where moths and vermin do not destroy, and where thieves do not break in and steal. For where your treasure is, there your heart will be also" (Matt. 6:19–21).

There is much training to do every day while we are still here on this earth. Yes, sometimes the training is tough, and you will have hurdles to jump and many distractions along the way. Yes, you will even get tired at times and want to give up. But you must keep going. You will have to discipline yourself to finish the race set before you.

The good news is that God is with you always, coaching you along the way. God has not set us up for failure. His plans are good and to prosper us because we are so valuable to Him. I can hear Him say, "Come on and get up. Let's go; we have a lot to do today, and there are others who are valuable to Me, too, who don't know Me yet."

So get ready and be enthusiastic. It's thrilling to know you're going to win with God's direction! Isn't that exciting? The Lord has amazing plans for you. I love to be used by God to bless others and bring them to the

Lord. My prayer is that you feel the same way, too. People are waiting for you to come across their path to help coach them along their journey. There is a great victory there not just for you and the other person, but for God, too! This is where God can move so breakthroughs happen.

> Therefore, since we are surrounded by such a great cloud of witnesses, let us throw off everything that hinders and the sin that so easily entangles. And let us run with perseverance the race marked out for us, fixing our eyes on Jesus, the pioneer and perfecter of faith. For the joy set before him he endured the cross, scorning its shame, and sat down at the right hand of the throne of God. (Heb. 12:1–2)

Once you have finished your race, your prize will be waiting for you. The final gift is the crown of victory and eternal life. Can you for just one moment, imagine with me? You are standing before Jesus, and with you to receive the prize are those whom you have helped or have helped you. The race was so worth this very moment. We will be standing there together as a crowd of witnesses in the very presence of God. This is the gift that will last forever, and it is not the end but just the beginning! See you there on that day!

Big hugs,
Papa God and Ashley

Eloi, Eloi, Lema Sabachthani

This was a final statement of Jesus on the cross before He took His last breath at Calvary, "Eloi, Eloi, lema sabachthani?"

On a journey to understand this statement, I did some research in the Word and discovered that this phrase in Mark 15:34 and Matthew 27:46 means "My God, My God, why have you forsaken me?"

Since I am not Jewish, I did not understand it at first glance because it seems like Jesus is saying, "Why, God, did You leave me to die?" I knew that could not be right since Jesus came to earth in a human body for the purpose of dying in our place. In my heart, I knew this statement had a very important message but somehow has been misunderstood. But for a Jewish man or woman watching Jesus take His last breath, it would make complete sense since Jesus was the awaited promise foretold by Old Testament prophets which was being fulfilled right before their very eyes.

While I was spending time with Papa God and reading about the crucifixion, the Holy Spirit revealed that Jesus was not asking a question; it was a quote from Psalm 22:1 that King David (Jesus' forbearer) wrote, prophesying about Jesus on the cross. It was shown to me that Jesus was expressing the agony of taking the sin of the whole world on His body and the separation from God that was to take place for a short period of time. When He descended into hell, it was the first time Jesus would be without His Father. When thinking about it like that, I can feel why Jesus would say this. When I was running from God and in sin, I was miserable. I had unexplainable feelings of loneliness. When I wasn't living for God because of my sins, I felt separated from Him; I don't ever want to go back to that old way of life without the presence of God. Not being able to hear His voice is a difficult way to live. Life without God's presence is hopelessness and darkness. I prefer His hope and light! It is that connection with God that gives us peace and life with an incredible gift to love. Scripture says that Jesus descended into the lower regions of the earth, "into hell," which is spiritual separation from God. (See Eph. 4:9, Acts 2:24, Col. 2:15.) This, of course, spurred me to hunt for more answers from Psalm 22 to see if David prophesied what was to come of Jesus on the cross centuries before the crucifixion took place.

To my pleasant surprise, I found more than I had expected. It goes into details from the birth of Jesus, to the mocking people in the hours leading up to the cross, to being disjointed from his bones, to being left naked with the shame of the world placed upon Him. It even describes His dominion and how the unborn will proclaim His righteousness. This means the future generations after the resurrection of Jesus. The best part was to come in the end of the chapter when the Scripture said, "He has done it!" "For dominion belongs to the LORD and he rules over the nations. All the rich of the earth will feast and worship; all who go down to the dust will kneel before him—those who cannot keep themselves alive. Posterity will serve him; future generations will be told about the Lord. They will proclaim his righteousness, declaring to a people yet unborn: He has done it!" (Ps. 22:28–31).

That is so amazing to me. So have I captured your interest yet?

Good! Go read all of Psalm 22 for yourself. I want you to see this, too. When reading about this, think about Jesus hanging on the cross in detail and how God knew beforehand when this most amazing event would take place in the history of mankind. He knew He had to sacrifice royal blood (both physically and spiritually) in order to take our place in sin and death. The cool part is He gave David, Jesus' forbearer, the words to speak of this fulfillment.

Take the time to listen to what the Lord is saying to you in these next verses and think about how Jesus conquered death and rose again just for you. He is now seated in the holiest place in heaven. He sat down knowing He had done what He needed to do for His beloved (you and me), and it was finished once and for all.

No longer would a human priest need to enter the temple and go behind the curtain once a year with the blood of an animal sacrificed by mortal man. The animal sacrifice was only atonement, a covering for the sin. It couldn't then and doesn't now take away sins.

Jesus was that spotless sacrifice who took away the sin of every person who has lived and who will live, destroying the bondage of our sins Satan had held mankind captive to for so long. With this, Jesus became our High Priest, not made by human hands.

The Blood of Christ

But when Christ came as high priest of the good things that are now already here, he went through the greater and more perfect tabernacle that is not made with human hands, that is to say, is not a part of this creation. He did not enter by means of the blood of goats and calves; but he entered the Most Holy Place once for all by his own blood, thus obtaining eternal redemption. The blood of goats and bulls and the ashes of a heifer sprinkled on those who are ceremonially unclean sanctify them so that they are outwardly clean. How much more, then, will the blood of Christ, who through the eternal Spirit offered himself unblemished to God, cleanse our consciences from acts that lead to death, so that we may serve the living God! (Heb. 9:11–14)

As our High Priest, Jesus made a way for us to die to sin and be born again spiritually by the power of His blood and resurrection. For a mortal man, death apart from God is eternal separation from Him. Again, that is why there is a hell. It always amazes me that anytime I have ever brought up hell to unbelievers or lukewarm "Christians," they start acting very strange and they get all squirmy on me. They can't understand that if God is a loving God, why and exactly how could He send people to a place that is full of torment?

God is a loving God, but He is also justice and truth, making Him a good judge. The better question would be to ask why He would allow sin and rebellion into heaven.

What they do not understand is that hell is separation from God; He is not there. It wasn't made for human beings; it was designed for fallen angels and for Lucifer. It is eternal damnation for their rebellion against Him. God is light and life, so sin is a separation from light into death and darkness. (See Heb. 9:11–14.) Do you recall what God did prior to creating the earth? He separated light and dark, and He saw that the light was good. (See Gen. 1:4.)

God doesn't want anyone going to hell but we must choose—life or death, sin or forgiveness. We must accept Jesus as our Lord and Savior for our names to be listed in the Lamb's Book of Life. "Nothing impure will ever enter it, nor will anyone who does what is shameful or deceitful, but only those whose names are written in the Lamb's book of life" (Rev. 21:27).

What shocks me the most is when the subject of hell comes up, people are in denial or stubborn to believe a lie, and they don't want to talk about it. The very place they are afraid of is the place they don't want to learn about. It doesn't make any sense to me to avoid the topic. I want to know about how to avoid going there instead of avoiding knowing about it. If someone told you to jump in a truck and didn't tell you where they were taking you, wouldn't you avoid jumping into that truck? I mean, duh! Wouldn't it be logical to research the destination first and know who the person is and their character, even if that person told you where they were going and the route they would take?

Listen very carefully: Choosing to ignore the facts is still choosing. People are sent to eternal damnation for choosing to reject Jesus and truth. Jesus spoke of hell more than He spoke of heaven. There must be a reason He spoke of this place so much. He wanted to warn us there is such a place, and He wanted us to choose life.

Listed below are some of the Scriptures I found pertaining to hell, gnashing of teeth, the lake of fire, and eternal death. Do your own homework on this and research the answers from God before you make a final decision on what you believe or don't believe.

Psalm 37:20, 69:28
Malachi 4:1
Matthew 5:22, 5:29–30, 10:28, 13:42, 18:9, 23:15
Mark 9:43–47
Luke 12:5, 13:22–28
John 5:24
Romans 5:21, 6:23
Hebrews 9:14
James 3:6
2 Peter 2:4–9
Revelation 20

Without repentance from sin, we are spiritually dead in our sins. Remember in our previous chapters that Adam fell and took on Satan's sinful nature? Adam no longer had the nature of God or zoe life in him. My dad, Pastor Darrell Morgan, calls people who are not born again, "the walking dead." They seem to be alive because in the natural realm they walk, talk, sleep, and can reason, but they do not have the Spirit of God in them so they are walking around spiritually dead inside. That is why when we ask Jesus to be our Lord, we have a spiritual death of the person we used to be. That old man of sin changes, and our eyes are opened to Jesus and what He accomplished on the cross for us. This spiritual awakening brings us back into fellowship with God; it removes the veil of deception from our understanding. There is no longer a separation from Him with us. Eternal life is in the blood of Jesus. "But if we walk in the light, as he is in the light, we have fellowship with one another, and the blood of Jesus, his Son, purifies us from all sin" (1 John 1:7).

Think about that. Our hearts must beat and pump blood through our physical bodies for us to stay alive. The blood of Jesus is what keeps us alive spiritually. Since Jesus lives in the heart of every believer, His Spirit is alive on the inside of us. Oh, man! Chew on that for a few minutes! That's good!

With forgiveness from God, we are then born again spiritually, bringing on His very spiritual nature and life and giving us dominion through Christ Jesus to rule and reign on this earth with the power of His name.

Just like when a woman is married, she takes on her husband's name. We, the church, are the bride of Christ.

I pray that the eyes of your heart may be enlightened in order that you may know the hope to which he has called you, the riches of his glorious inheritance in his holy people, and his incomparably great power for us who believe. That power is the same as the mighty strength he exerted when he raised Christ from the dead and seated him at his right hand in the heavenly realms, far above all rule and authority, power and dominion, and every name that is invoked, not only in the present age but also in the one to come. And God placed all things under his feet and appointed him to be head over everything for the church, which is his body, the fullness of him who fills everything in every way. (Eph. 1:18–23)

This inheritance is a free gift to us if we will believe it and accept it. Never forget who you are and the price that was paid to bring you back in fellowship with our Creator. Your life and His life aren't for nothing. There is a purpose to everything God does, and He gave us historical and documented proof beforehand. How is this not proof enough for doubters?

Jesus fulfilled all the Old Testament prophecy of His birth, death, and resurrection. Based on my research, Jesus fulfilled 353 prophecies.[6] I think it would be difficult for someone to fulfill three prophecies and impossible for someone to try to fulfill 353. I have even heard from others that there were more than just these. Even if there are more, this alone should be our proof that Jesus is who He says He is. He fulfilled His promise to us, and there are yet more prophecies to be fulfilled when He returns for His bride. Praise God, we are not deserted or forsaken! Spiritual death could not hold Him in the grave, and it cannot hold us, for Jesus has done it! We are no longer forsaken.

Big hugs,
Papa God and Ashley

---

6   http://www.accordingtotheScriptures.org/prophecy/353prophecies.html

Glowing in the Dark

The Lord has been showing me how as Christians we literally carry His light around in us.

I had once heard a prophet say, "In the spirit realm, Christians glow." She referred to us as "walking lights." She said, "This is how demonic spirits are able to tell who are children of God and who are still in darkness." When I heard this, the Lord started giving me examples of this light, and on several different occasions, the Holy Spirit showed me how it worked.

The first example came on a day I had been traveling for work and listening to Christian music while driving around my car. I could feel the glory of God with me, and it was such a joyful time in the Lord's presence. (If you ever see me driving down the road and singing, know that I am singing to God and praising Him. Don't laugh at me, just join in). Smile!

It was at lunch time, and so I stopped by the grocery store to grab a sandwich. As I walked through the store this man stopped me and said, "Wow! There is something about you that is different. It's like you literally are glowing."

Thinking quickly, I laughed and said, "It's Jesus in me that you see."

He looked at me funny and then smiled and said, "Oh my, um, yes. Praise God!"

I think he was trying to flirt with me because I could feel his intentions were not trustworthy, and my words stopped him dead in his tracks. I could see a conviction on his face after I had made my proclamation. Ha! I love how God works.

A few weeks later it happened again in the grocery store near my home. This time, it was a lady waiting near me at the deli counter. She looked at me kindly and said, "I hope this doesn't seem weird to say but you are glowing with a light around you."

I told her the same thing I told the man at the other grocery store, "It's Jesus in me that you see."

She looked at me and said, "Wow! Yes, I can see that!"

Surprisingly, this continued to happen to me on a few other occasions, and I knew the Lord was showing me something about this light in me. If anything, it was a way to witness to others about the Lord without being pushy. After all, they were the ones who mentioned the light to me.

One night, I woke up with a ton of stress because of a certain situation in my life. Thoughts were running over and over in my head and were keeping me awake. I prayed and said, "Lord, I know You told me not to worry, and I am trying my best to give this situation to You, but these thoughts keep replaying in my mind and are not letting me sleep."

The Lord reminded me of 1 John 4:4 KJV, one of my favorite Scriptures: "Greater is He that is in you, than he that is in the world." This Scripture is one I have stood on for many years, but God was about to show it to me in a whole new way.

Again, the Lord then reminded me of what the prophet had said, "In the spirit realm, Christians glow." I realized that the times my light seemed to glow brighter and others could see this light was when I was in the presence of God. I still find it amazing that His light was shining so brightly in me that others could see it.

As I lay there in the dark, the Lord started to show me how this light works against the enemy. The Holy Spirit gave me wisdom and understanding pertaining to this light. Imagine sitting in a dark room and someone points a flashlight directly in your eyes. What would your reaction be? You would try to cover your eyes and protect them from the bright light, right? In John 8:12, Jesus says, "I am the light of the world." Knowing this to be truth, do you remember 1 John 4:4? Greater is He who *lives in me* than he who is in the world. So then, if Jesus lives in you and in me as believers of the gospel, then His light shines in us and through us. We then reflect His light in the darkness.

Suddenly, I knew exactly what to do! I thought about Jesus and imagined Him living in my body. Then I said, "Jesus reflect." Suddenly, in the spirit realm, I could see a bright light envelop and radiate around me, lighting up the darkness. (That is the only way I could describe it.) It covered the sphere of where I was lying on my bed. After this, the thoughts replaying over and over in my head amazingly stopped, and I went back to sleep.

The Lord showed me that demons cannot stand that light and they must flee because of the name of Jesus. That light shining brightly in me is so bright that it hurts their eyes. Praise God!

I thought this was cool, so anytime I have thoughts I know are not of God like fear, defeat, anger, or depression, I practice this maneuver on the enemy. I must have been practicing this so much that I looked like a lightbulb walking around in the spirit realm. I heard a saying once that goes like this: "Thoughts of fear mean there is a demon near." Fear is not of God so tell the demon to get lost in the name of Jesus. I've literally told Satan, "You just keep it up because you and your minions will hate coming near me with those lies. I'm just going to keep blinding you with the light of Jesus in me."

While reading this response to the enemy, can you see me smile? Well, I do, and I smile really big because I know who my God is, and Satan has already been defeated! I don't say this with a rude undertone; I say it with complete confidence in what Jesus did for me by conquering sin and death on the cross.

The Lord was not yet finished teaching me about this light. One day, while I was at a trade show for work, I saw this man walking down the open hallway between a long line of trade show booths. He had long brown hair and was dressed kind of rough. This is not a big deal to me because I don't care if someone is dressed up or dressed down; I just love people, and I enjoy talking to them.

As I stood there, I tried to get his attention and say hello. When I looked at his face, I noticed he had something on his forehead that looked like a black star. He was walking toward a group of people standing in the center of the hallway, and all of a sudden, his body turned to walk toward me. It seemed as though it was unknown to him at first that I was standing there, yet he was drawn over to me. When he looked up at me, he screamed, "Ahhh!" As he screamed, he threw his hands up in front of his eyes to obstruct his view, blocking what seemed to be a great light reflection. Then he turned away and walked over to his friends and carried on what seemed to be a normal conversation.

Now, if I were on one of those hidden camera TV shows, I probably would have won the million dollars. My face told the whole story of shock. It was the most peculiar thing, and I could not believe what I had just experienced. Seriously, it was like something out of a creepy movie. I later found out that the star on his head was a pentagram, a star of Satan.

When I got home, I went on a hunt in the Bible for Scriptures that talk about this light in us. There are so many that I can't possibly put them all down. So I found a few that I believe relate to the light of Jesus living in the believers.

In him was life, and that life was the light of all mankind. The light shines in the darkness, and the darkness has not overcome it. (John 1:4–5)

You are the light of the world. A town built on a hill cannot be hidden. Neither do people light a lamp and put it under a bowl. Instead, they put it on its stand, and it gives light to everyone in the house. In the same way, let your light shine before others, that they may see your good deeds and glorify your Father in heaven. (Matt. 5:14–16)

Think about how the book of Genesis starts out. With that thought in mind, let's look to see what was the first command God gave over this earth that we live in? "Now the earth was formless and empty, darkness was over the surface of the deep, and the Spirit of God was hovering over the waters. And God said, "Let there be light," and there was light. God saw that the light was good, and he separated the light from the darkness" (Gen. 1:2–3).

Do you see where the Holy Spirit is leading us? God is light and life. Our bodies are the temple of the Holy Spirit, and His Spirit abides in us. "Don't you know that you yourselves are God's temple and that God's Spirit dwells in your midst?" (1 Cor. 3:16).

Come on! This is good. I hope you are getting as excited about this as I am! Think about it like this: God is supernatural, therefore we have a super power, the power of the Holy Spirit. If you grew up anything like I did, you always wanted to be a superhero. Woo hoo! My sister Che' and I would play like superheroes when we were little girls. Well, now you know that you are! This light in us is our guide, our strength, and this super power comes with joy and wisdom beyond what the world sees or knows. The closer we are in spirit with our Creator, the bigger that light glows. That's awesome! The Lord also reminded me of a song we used to sing in vacation Bible school when I a little girl called, "This Little Light of Mine."

I have said all of this to tell you: Do not allow the enemy to blow out the light shining in you. God gave you this light to spread to others just as you would share a lit candle with others in the darkness so they, too, could see and not stumble.

This light comes with a warning. If you try to use it with any anger, frustration, or in vindication, the light will not work. It is not a false light. Remember, God is love. He is a good God full of love and mercy. He will never allow us to use His light as a weapon against others. Satan will try to use anything in his arsenal of weapons, but he cannot use God's light. That light is a gift for us to use for God's glory only.

I encourage you to keep singing to our God and worship Him for who He is and what He has done for you. You will notice that the light in you will glow brighter and brighter as you love on Papa God and glorify His Son with your words and actions. Jesus lives in you, so let your light glow brightly for all to see. This light is a witness to those still in the dark. Many are seeking this light but may not know how to attain it. Let them find the answer in you.

Just like the man at my trade show, the light might scare some because they are afraid of it and are so deep in the darkness they literally scream at you and walk away. But don't let that stop you from being the light God called you to be in this world. There is a purpose for your life and Papa God intentionally gave you this light to lead others to His Son.

When the enemy tries to tell you his lies, fight back with that light inside of you. Trust me on this, he hates it! I can't help but light up with a smile every time I think about this revelation, and I hope it helps you like it helped me.

We are all individual lights all over the world and if we stand together as one body of Christ, this light will shine even brighter for all to see like a city on the hill. "You are the light of the world. A town built on a hill cannot be hidden" (Matt. 5:14).

Let it shine. Let it shine. Let it shine! Ready? Glow!

Big hugs,
Papa God and Ashley

Grudge or Mercy

When in a disagreement with someone, it so easy to shut down our feelings and hold a grudge especially when we have been hurt by the other person. Words have been said that just can't be taken back, words that cut like a knife to the core of your heart and mind. Those harsh words can hurt even more when we are the most vulnerable, when we're at our weakest moment. It may seem like those words are kicking us down even when we think we just can't get any lower.

To make matters worse, the enemy comes in and whispers even more lies that continue the beating after the battle of words has long passed. If we're not careful, thoughts of anger and hate can creep into the wounded heart. Soon the molehill becomes a mountain of volcanic action.

So what does God say about what to do while in a disagreement with another? "Therefore, confess your sins to each other and pray for each other so that you may be healed. The prayer of a righteous person is powerful and effective" (James 5:16).

Here are a few things I have learned over the years whether it be a disagreement with family, friends, or in a work environment.

First, go to Papa God and pray about the situation and for the other person. Pray that the Lord intervenes with wisdom and strength. Also, if your thoughts are totally out of control with anger, pray for yourself as well. I believe people forget to pray for themselves. It's really important to do that because it gets the me, me, me under control. And ask God if you are the one in the wrong, so you can make the situation right. There will be times we are the one in the right and times we are not. Being humble is important to keep our hearts right with God and others. I am not sure who said we always have to be the one in the right. If that were the case, there wouldn't be wars, divorces, and separations. This is selfishness rooted in pride. Pride is setting our own selfish motives above God's plans for His kingdom. This is exactly what Lucifer did before he was booted out heaven because he wanted to be God. (See Isa. 14:15, Ezek. 28:16–17.) We must be sure we aren't making this same mistake as Adam and Eve did by allowing deception and pride to creep in.

Second, ask God for peace of mind. Pray that His thoughts and words are your thoughts and words. Get your Bible out and ask the Holy Spirit to teach you in His Word what He wants you to learn. This experience may be the lesson needed to move you up to the next level in your spiritual walk with God and others. Pray for understanding and what to say and do moving forward.

It is OK to back away from the situation until you can gather your emotions and hear what the Lord wants you to do next. There is nothing wrong with a little space in the middle of a disagreement. But don't stay in isolation for too long. Nothing good happens in isolation. There is only loneliness, and nothing is solved alone. Isolation causes hearts to be hardened and that's not God's way of healing; it's a tactic of the enemy.

It is so important to confront the situation and confess your sins to the other person without pointing fingers. Remember, in an argument, each person believes they are in the right at that moment.

With the guidance and help of the Holy Spirit, you can face anything with which the enemy tries to beat you down. When you have heard from the Lord, speak in love and confidence, knowing that God is with you. The enemy's goal is to conquer and divide. If Satan can cause separation with family and friends, he has won the battle.

God is *love*, so we too must walk in love. If we are not walking in love, then we are not acting like God; we are acting like the enemy.

> Above all, love each other deeply, because love covers over a multitude of sins. Offer hospitality to one another without grumbling. Each of you should use whatever gift you have received to serve others, as faithful stewards of God's grace in its various forms. If anyone speaks, they should do so as one who speaks the very words of God. If anyone serves, they should do so with the strength God provides, so that in all things God may be praised through Jesus Christ. To him be the glory and the power forever and ever. Amen. (1 Peter 4:8–11)

Really listening to each other is important. The point behind an argument is not to be right but to be understood and find a resolution. Most arguments are just a misunderstanding and can be mixed with insecurities. There is nothing worse than the feeling of not being heard. As a woman, I believe that's mostly what women want anyway, to be heard. Obviously, I am not a man, but what I have observed in many situations is that men like to close up their emotions, go silent, and have the attitude of, "Just do what I say and what you're told." For women: Just don't rant on; that will get you nowhere. Trust me on this one. Neither of these situations is healthy. Bottled up anger and continual vented frustration ultimately not only affect the relationship, but the health of our bodies when toxic words and anger are held inside us.

I will tell on myself. One day I was sitting in my office working when a co-worker who was in a bad mood and frustrated walked in the room. This person started yelling at me and screamed all kinds of unkind words. Right before that person walked out of the room, they ended their rant with words that hit the core of my gut.

I jumped up out of my seat to go after them, and I heard the Holy Spirit say, "Sit down, Ashley, and say nothing!" I sat right back down, but I wasn't happy about it. I must have looked like a big baby with a grumpy face and my arms crossed.

I recall being really frustrated by this command by God, and I said back to Him in my thoughts, "You are not going to allow this person to talk to me that way, are You?"

Then the Lord said, "I will tell you what to say when you calm down. But when you speak, say only what I tell you to say." Talk about a spiritual spanking from Papa God! It was a double whammy on my ego!

I knew in my heart that God was right. So I prayed and asked Him to help me to not hold a grudge and show me how to forgive. When I heard what God wanted me to say and I got my heart right with Him, I waited about twenty minutes before I approached this person. I walked in calmly and spoke in an even-toned voice, "I am not sure why you are having a bad day, but I want to tell you that I am sorry you are so unhappy today. I do hope your day gets better. With that said, I did not deserve what was spoken to me, but I forgive you anyway." Then I walked away peacefully. Amazingly, about thirty minutes later, the apology came.

This story isn't about a person or even the argument. This story is about Jesus and how God loves this person just as much as He loves Jesus. For me personally, this story was about my obedience to the voice of God and controlling my flesh. I realize now that it was an example on how to forgive.

That leads us to a good question. How much does God love Jesus? I hope you would say a whole lot. How much does God love you? A whole lot! Walking in love is the only way God can get to someone who is being ugly. Do you understand that? God isn't out to get people for being ugly. He wants their hearts, and if He can use the heart of Jesus who is living in me, He will. And I am willing to be used by God. God is mercy, and He asks us to be like Him. Who am I to hold a grudge against anyone?

Here is something to strongly consider. If the person you are in a disagreement with doesn't know Jesus as their Lord and Savior, don't be surprised that they aren't being kind. This is because they don't have zoe life in them. You can't expect them to act like Jesus when they don't have the love and life of God living inside them. This is when you start praying for their salvation and taking authority over the enemy in their life. Pray that no weapon formed against you will prosper in the name of Jesus. (See Isa. 54:17.)

If the person is saved, then your prayer is that God shows them or you what needs to be corrected.

We all have bad days occasionally, and honestly, this happens to a lot of people. I know it has happened to me on more than one occasion, and I must say that I am really impressed with myself for being obedient to God on how I handled this disagreement. Just because I am a Christian doesn't mean I can't make mistakes or wish I hadn't said something that I would love to take back. One very important point I do want to tell you is that our words change things. They can heal, or they can destroy. We have the choice on how to use them. Our tongues will control where we go, and their effects are striking on others, producing results that lead us on our journey in life. James said it like this:

> We all stumble in many ways. Anyone who is never at fault in what they say is perfect, able to keep their whole body in check. When we put bits into the mouths of horses to make them obey us, we can turn the whole animal. Or take ships as an example. Although they are so large and are driven by strong winds, they are steered by a very small rudder wherever the pilot wants to go. Likewise, the tongue is

a small part of the body, but it makes great boasts. Consider what a great forest is set on fire by a small spark. (James 3:2–5)

We must be careful with our words so that we don't set fires we can't put out. Our words carry great power. After all, God's words are what created the universe we live in and all that is in it and beyond. The same principle applies to people; our words literally change the atmosphere around us.

This is why we must carefully think before we say something that may be hurtful, especially with children. Children take things literally. They don't have the maturity and wisdom to process and filter out words that are harmful.

On the positive side, sometimes a disagreement isn't such a bad thing amongst mature adults. It gets the truth out in the open, and that is where healing begins and resolution can move things in the right direction. We just have to learn how to control our emotions and our words to be most effective.

My mom is a very wise lady. She once told me something I will never forget, and I try to apply this method to difficult conversations. She said, "Build up the conversation like a sandwich. Start with a word of praise, then add the meat of the matter, and end it with a slice of praise." This implies that if we want to be understood so that a positive change can be made, we should first say something kind, then say what we need to say in truth and love, and then end on a positive note.

Insults don't work. They just lead to more frustration, hurt feelings, and separation.

Oh, and for heaven's sake, never try to have a serious discussion when you're over-tired and/or hungry. You can't think clearly and logically when you're tired and hungry. My daughter calls that being hangry—hungry and angry at the same time. If you add aggravated, you're in trouble, and you just need to walk away nicely.

When we hold a grudge, the only person we are hurting is ourselves. If we approach the other person in love and try to resolve the issue, we are being obedient to God. If we hold the grudge and say rude things back, there is no peace in that.

Keep in mind that it is important to set reasonable boundaries. If the other person does not want to comply with you, it's OK. Don't take on their burden.

You made the attempt to try to resolve the matter and just maybe more time is needed to think. God gave each of us one of the greatest gifts we have ever been given, free will. If there is love and respect, the other person will eventually come back around. "If it is possible, as far as it depends on you, live at peace with everyone" (Rom. 12:18).

There will always be some form of opposition in our lives. What matters is how we handle that opposition and what we do next. Don't allow strife to rule your life. It shows great strength and maturity when you try to resolve the situation instead of trying to hurt the other person back.

The last step in resolving the issue is to think of and write down all the wonderful things the other person has done right. I personally have come up with at least five things that person does that help my life and the lives of others. If you can think of more, great. Write them down. Sometimes when we are focusing our attention on the good things, those good qualities will out-weigh the wrongs. Start saying nice things about that person, and you will see that not only your heart will change toward them, you will see a heart change in that person, too. They will see something in you that makes them want what you have, a relationship with Jesus.

Listen, it's even OK to agree to disagree, but at least the conversation was had in the first place. Be respectful even if someone doesn't see things the way you see them. Everyone is allowed to have their own opinion as long as it doesn't harm someone in the process. The most important part of the story is to see this person the way God sees them. If you pray and give the situation to God, He will fight your battles for you so that you don't have to get upset over what someone said to you or about you. Pray with a pure heart that God will expose the wrong and bring a resolution that gives Him glory. If you are following the promptings of the Holy Spirit, love already abides in you, and the Lord will work it all out for His glory and goodness. God's mercy is freedom and what breaks the power of the grudge or anger. Stay in peace, knowing it will all work out the way the Lord intended. Be forgiving and love mercy over judgment. In the end, what matters is that is Papa God is glorified, not ourselves.

Big hugs,
Papa God and Ashley

Do You Trust Me?

I used to battle with asthma, and it would lead to severe anxiety if I did not have a rescue inhaler with me. Then there were many times that anxiety brought on the asthma attacks. It's like one symptom ruled another symptom, and learned behavior would start to take over because of fear. It was a vicious cycle that became out of control when I allowed it.

I had been in the hospital several times with asthma in my youth. I remember all too well how it felt to be helpless and going to the ER with the symptoms of suffocation. If I had an attack, I would take my inhaler and try to calm myself down in an effort to avoid the hospital. If I got worse, my whole body would go numb, and my lips would even start to tingle. This was a terrible feeling, and as the years passed, I really wanted to be free from it.

I prayed and prayed that God would heal me. I knew all the Scriptures on healing, and I would quote them to myself to feel better. Nine times out of ten, I would feel better when I prayed, but my dependence on an inhaler never left, and the symptoms would return.

In 2011, God called me out of my comfort zone, and in faith, I started my own company. It was my first time venturing out on my own, and I was very nervous. My nerves would get the better of me, and it would cause me tremendous anxiety. It felt like I had an elephant sitting on my chest. Even when I spoke, you could hear my shortness of breath. My husband would say, "Ashley, you need to relax; you're making me anxious when you speak because of your shortness of breath." That is when I fully understood that this had moved past asthma into full-blown anxiety.

One day I sat on my couch and prayed, "God, I know that You are my healer. I need Your help to understand and believe what Your Word really means when You said, 'By His wounds, we are healed.'" "But he was pierced for our transgressions, he was crushed for our iniquities; the punishment that brought us peace was on him, and by his wounds, we are healed" (Isa. 53:5).

Suddenly, I heard God say in my spirit, "My Son Jesus has already taken your sickness and anxiety on His body on the cross, but the problem is you don't really trust Me to heal you."

Shocked and feeling a little deflated by this response, I knew I had not been faithful with what the Word of God tells me and what Jesus did for me. I said, "I thought I trusted You, God, but I realize now that I really have not up to this point." I proceeded to confess my lack of faith. And so I said out loud with a confident and more renewed declaration, "Yes, Lord, I do trust You now."

Once I said those words, *whoosh!* (That word is the only way I can describe the feeling that took over.) I could feel that air had immediately filled my lungs. I thought, "Wow! How did that happen? I can breathe again!" In my amazement and appreciation for what just happened, I praised God and went on about my day.

The next afternoon, I began to worry, and I felt short of breath again. So I prayed and said, "God, I know you were teaching me something yesterday with trust. Speak to me again."

Then I heard God say in my spirit, "Do you really trust Me, Ashley?"

I said, "Yes Lord, I do trust You." Then it happened again, whoosh! Instantly I could feel that air filled my lungs, and I could breathe again. My chest felt lighter, and I could breathe without effort! I started to thank God and was very excited about what just happened.

I wish I could say that I was healed from that exact minute, but I wasn't. God and I had to go over this for about two weeks, every day and sometimes several times a day. I know now what I was going through during this time was that I was exercising my faith. Faith is like a muscle. You must build it up and work on it daily to get healthy. With every declaration of my faith, God was showing me that every time I said, "God, I trust You," I could then breathe again without effort and medication.

I finally started to trust God so much that I threw my inhaler in the trash can in my garage. The funny part is that was it was Monday when I threw my inhaler away, but the garbage truck wouldn't come again until the middle of the week. The inhaler sat in the trash can for a few days before it would be gone. With this action of faith, God was taking me to a new level of trust. This was a big leap of faith for me, and I thought to myself, "If I can do this, then I know I am delivered."

As gross as this may sound, during this long week, I would feel breathless and find myself going out to the garage to literally dig in the trash can to find the inhaler. In those moments, I felt that I could not live without it, and I needed it to breathe again. It was a habit and an addiction I had learned over many years of dependence. The inhaler seemed to have some sort of control over me, and I even felt at times that it was taunting me to get it out of the trash to use it.

God stopped me in my tracks every time I attempted to get it out. While walking to the garage, He would repeat the question to me, "Ashley, do you trust Me?"

My answer was always, "Yes, Papa God, I do trust You." Then suddenly, whoosh! The air would fill my lungs, and I would walk away from that trash can because I knew I did not need the rescue inhaler.

Then the big test day arrived. Before I knew it, it was trash day, and the garbage truck came barreling loudly down the street. I knew this was it. My faith was being tested like never before. I recall thinking, "Do I run and get that inhaler before they take it away, or do I trust God?" Now it was up to me to stand strong on what I knew to be the truth and to trust God completely.

I started reminding myself, "Yes, I do trust God as my healer, and I don't need that medication to help me breathe anymore." I prayed, "God I really do trust that You have me in Your hands, and that You will not lead me into a path that would harm me. You have already proven that I can breathe with Your help over the past few weeks. Every time I told You that I trusted You, I could suddenly breathe again, and now, God, I really do believe You and trust You. I release asthma and anxiety to You in Jesus' name. Amen."

The dump truck stopped in front of my house and picked up my garbage can and dumped it into its big compartments, taking my inhaler away from me. I could hear the engines of the truck driving down the street, and it was an exhilarating feeling. I knew I had won this battle with the power and help of the Holy Spirit.

It was scary for me to take that step of faith. I still get tears in my eyes when I read this story to myself because it was a turning point in my life; I had fully trusted the Lord. I am just so grateful to be free from dependence on those inhalers. I no longer need them, and I no longer call them "my inhalers." They don't belong to me anymore, and so I do not claim ownership over them. Praise God!

Up until a year after, I still had those moments that I felt breathless, and anxiety would try to creep its ugly head in again, but I knew immediately what I was supposed to do. I would just say those wonderful words, "Papa God, I trust You." Air would fill my lungs, and I would be off doing what I needed to do that day. I haven't looked back since. I can boldly claim that I am delivered.

Trusting and believing God are two key components in setting us free from whatever has us bound. Maybe for you, it is an illness, anxiety, or an addiction. God wants to set you free from that today. We can pray all day long and memorize all the Scriptures, but until we literally trust and believe the Word of God, we will keep going around and around with God on those same hindrances and defeats. Jesus already paid the price. We just have to accept His free gift of freedom. That is where faith and action step in and take over. "Those who know your name trust in you, for you, LORD, have never forsaken those who seek you" (Ps. 9:10).

Whatever battle you are going through right now, pray about it and ask God what to do, then follow the promptings of the Holy Spirit. I am confident that He will tell you. Then keep your eyes on Jesus. He will teach you and show you how to conquer those things that have you bound. He loves you so much and is ready to set you free.

Now God is passing this question on to you. He is asking, "Do you trust Me?"

If you do, get ready to be free! God will never fail you, and He is always trustworthy.

Big hugs,
Papa God and Ashley

Value Life

It is no secret that I am a huge advocate for promoting life. After all, I stand up and speak at various events advocating for children looking for their forever homes and child sponsorships through Holt International. With all my speaking engagements for Holt, I have been praying and seeking the Lord about the number of abortions in this country happening as we speak.

My heart is troubled by the lack of concern the people of this country have for this matter. I have been asking God why so many people are turning a blind eye to the helpless, the innocent, and the suffering. Yes, there are those who stand up for life and truth, yet the laborers are way too few for the volume of these innocent lives taken without their consent, and this is more than concerning.

When I asked God to show me His heart on this subject, He said, "How can My people, who I created to love, love others if they don't love and honor Me, and they don't value and love themselves?" Wow! That's another spiritual spanking if I've ever heard one. Did you feel it?

Since Roe v. Wade was legalized in 1973—Jane Roe, a twenty-one-year old pregnant woman and Henry Wade, the United States Attorney

General—from February 1973 to February 2016, approximately 58 million unborn babies have been aborted in America. That's about 3,000 abortions per day in the US alone. Worldwide there have been 1,405,247,312 and climbing just since 1980.[7] For your own education, I urge you to go look up how much this number has increased since I wrote this. You will be shocked! Those numbers are astounding, and frankly, I am shocked by them. In 2016, the media uncovered that a well-known abortion agency was selling body parts of these defenseless babies.

What in the heck is wrong with people? Aren't we more precious to God than this? Where has the heart of this nation gone? We riot when someone is shot in the streets (innocent or not), but way too few stand up and protest about those 58 million innocent lives? What did these babies do to deserve this? Where was their choice to live? Do their lives even matter? Yes, *all* lives matter! Oh, my heart is pained just at the thought of it. Even women who profess the name of Jesus are walking into abortion clinics and holding a cross in their hands as these poor babies' little legs and arms are being ripped apart and thrown in the garbage like an old and useless rag.

Do we really think that God hasn't taken notice of these babies filling up heaven before they had a chance at life? Deception is running rampant, and it must be stopped through awareness and repentance.

I know. I can hear it now, "I have the right to choose, and you have no idea why I feel abortion is justifiable."

My answer back to you is, yes, you are correct, we all have a choice. We have a right to choose to do whatever we want. This is a gift from God to all of humanity. But I want to appeal to you to look at it this way: You can choose to sin or not to sin. Just because we have a choice doesn't mean God condones it. Freedom of speech is a constitutional right,

---

7   http://www.numberofabortions.com/
https://prochoice.org/education-and-advocacy/about-abortion/history-of-abortion/

but when it comes to what God says about abortion, freedom against the gift of life is not a biblical right. Scientifically, at conception, those cells come alive, and a human is growing with life, and body parts are forming. If it weren't true then the cells wouldn't multiply. I encourage you and others who have a hard time with this to check your conscience on this matter. Before someone reading this becomes unhinged, my plea is for you to continue to see this as caution, not as an attack. I want to remind you that I am yet only a simple messenger; please read what God says about choosing life or death in Holy Scripture. This way you aren't too offended because this comes from God Himself.

> See, I set before you today life and prosperity, death and destruction. For I command you today to love the LORD your God, to walk in obedience to him, and to keep his commands, decrees and laws; then you will live and increase, and the LORD your God will bless you in the land you are entering to possess. But if your heart turns away and you are not obedient, and if you are drawn away to bow down to other gods and worship them, I declare to you this day that you will certainly be destroyed. You will not live long in the land you are crossing the Jordan to enter and possess. This day I call the heavens and the earth as witnesses against you that I have set before you life and death, blessings and curses. Now choose life, so that you and your children may live and that you may love the LORD your God, listen to his voice, and hold fast to him. For the LORD is your life, and he will give you many years in the land he swore to give to your fathers, Abraham, Isaac, and Jacob. (Deut. 30:15–20)

Friend, please adhere to this word. Based on what Scripture says, there is a huge price to pay for being disobedient to God. I know it seems like I am being harsh, but if we are proclaiming Christians, we are called to stand up for the innocent. On the flip side of the coin, there is a great reward for choosing life. Think about it like this: God is in the life business while the condemner of our souls, the devil, is in the death business. Whose side are you on? Choose wisely because we will all have to give an account to God one day for our choices. "Speak up for those who cannot speak for themselves, for the rights of all who are destitute" (Prov. 31:8).

Have we fallen so far from a loving God who gave us His own life that we might be forgiven? Has God not said that He would never leave us or forsake us? Even in the valley of the shadow of death, He is with us. He said to fear no evil, and that He is with us. God's promises never change, and they never fail.

Here's a shocker for you. Imagine how the Virgin Mary felt when she had to explain her pregnancy to her betrothed husband who had yet to lay an intimate hand on her. How in the world could she explain to her parents that she was miraculously pregnant by the Holy Spirit without fearing rejection? Yet this unplanned pregnancy (unplanned by Mary) delivered the Savior of the world. Praise God! Warning! Young adults don't ever try to give this excuse to your parents; it only worked once. Smile!

Jesus wasn't a mistake, and neither is any other baby. Let's think beyond someone's current situation who has an unwanted pregnancy. What if the baby in question was the person God created to figure out a cure for some disease when they grew up? What if this medical breakthrough could have been the cure to help millions of people who would die without this cure? I am speaking theoretically of course. However, we will never know if that person isn't here to make a difference.

I want to go over a few other scenarios that are very important to consider. What if that child was the reason someone chooses to keep living life to the fullest? Without this child, there would be no joy that brought laughter on holidays and special occasions. Let's imagine that same joyful child who would grow up to then take care of their mom on her death bed. Without that child, that mom would live and die alone one day. Or apart from the birth mom, maybe that baby was the answer to someone's prayer of raising a child through adoption. There are plenty of families out there who have a desperate desire to have a child but cannot conceive. God had plans for this family to raise that child in a good home to accomplish His plans, but because the child was discarded, that great plan and prayer go unanswered.

I have even heard of a woman who could no longer conceive after an abortion. Though now married, she and her husband greatly wanted a child but couldn't because of what had happened years prior.

Oh, we can't forget to mention all the failed abortions that have left a child handicapped for the rest of their lives. Imagine how they feel growing up in society where they were once almost forbidden to live. That's a whole list of other emotional trauma for not only the child, but the parents as well. My sweet friend Chelsea is a product of a failed abortion. Can I just tell you how glad I am that she is alive today? Her smile lights up the room when she enters it. Chelsea walks on crutches, but those crutches can't stop that girl! She is thankful for the chance to live a life full of promise, and God uses her story for His glory.

We all make mistakes and fall short of the glory of God to sin, but a child is not a mistake. That child is a result of a decision made by two people to interact with one another intimately. I am not here to condemn anyone for having made the decision to abort their baby. That's between the individual and God. Going forward, what God is asking them to do is to go to Him, ask forgiveness, and to stand up for the innocent. I know there are other circumstances we aren't going to go into, but I think I have many several good points to consider.

Every life is precious to God. He loves each of us so much; we are His children and we are *all*, even the unborn, chosen by Him for His purpose. "For I know the plans I have for you," declares the Lord, "plans to prosper you and not to harm you, plans to give you hope and a future" (Jeremiah 29:11).

If you have supported abortion, or have had one yourself, now is the time to bring that to the feet of Jesus and ask for forgiveness. God is faithful to forgive. Once you ask for forgiveness, God remembers it no more. The enemy has no hold on you any longer once you have released your sin in prayer to God. Don't look back to that sin any longer. If you do, that's not God who is condemning you. Satan is the condemner of our souls. Tell him to take a hike in the name of Jesus. Because of the blood of Jesus, this is what God does with sin when we ask for forgiveness: "He does not treat us as our sins deserve or repay us according to our iniquities. For as high as the heavens are above the earth, so great is His love for those who fear him; as far as the east is from the west, so far has He removed our transgressions from us. As a father has compassion on his children, so the LORD has compassion on those who fear him" (Ps. 103:10–14).

Remember, you are so valuable and wonderfully made. God put a lot of thought into each one of His children even before we were born. He thought not only of the way we would look, but even down to our distinctive personalities. He knew exactly who we would be way before our parents knew about us and held us in their arms.

> For you created my inmost being; you knit me together in my mother's womb. I praise you because I am fearfully and wonderfully made; your works are wonderful, I know that full well. My frame was not hidden from you when I was made in the secret place, when I was woven together in the depths of the earth. Your eyes saw my unformed body; all the days ordained for me were written in your book before one of them came to be. How precious to me are your thoughts, God! How vast is the sum of them! (Ps. 139:13–17)

Oh, yes! God put a ton of thought into what you would be. It's time to start seeing yourself the way God sees you. Don't worry about what anyone else thinks about you or any mistakes that have been made. If you have asked the Lord to forgive you and show you who you are to Him, He is faithful. In the end, it only matters what God thinks and sees in you. If God values life, then shouldn't we value our own lives and the lives of others?

Jesus said that the greatest commandment is to love one another. This is how people will know we are His disciples. (See John 13:35.) Valuing ourselves and the lives of others allows us to be who we were created to be. You are not a mistake, and the mistakes that have been made are not too big for God to handle. Don't fall for that same lie that started way back in the Garden of Eden. Remember Satan's temptation of the forbidden fruit, "Did God really say that?" This is what Jesus said in John 10:10 "The thief [Satan] comes only to kill, steal and destroy; I have come so that you may have life and life to the full."

It is my prayer that this word from the Lord has opened your eyes to how important it is to stand up for the innocent and that you are set free from the way the world views life. "If you belonged to the world, it would love you as its own. As it is, you do not belong to the world, but I have chosen you out of the world. That is why the world hates you" (John 15:19).

I have a very important question for you that I want you to ponder. You are the main actress or actor in your life story. In the end, how will your story be told of the choices you made?

In conclusion, I want to remind you of something that my best friend, Nikki Robles, tells everyone after I have given a tough talk. She says, "God loves you very much!" And Nikki is correct, He does. His love is the reason that Jesus gave us His life.

Prayer: God, I choose life. Forgive me of my sins and wipe them away as far as the east is from the west. Whatever breaks Your heart, Lord, let it break my heart. Let me see people the way You see them, and let me see myself the way You see me, which is fearfully (thoughtfully) and wonderfully made. From this day forward, I will stand up for the innocent. I will show others how valuable they are to You and walk in Your love and compassion. I trust that You will work all things for my good. In Jesus' name, I pray. Amen.

If you or a family member have had an abortion, I truly believe that one day there will be a reunion with that child in heaven, and your embrace will be worth the wait.

Big hugs,
Papa God and Ashley

God Has Tentacles?

I have a separate mailbox for work that I check every so often. I have had this box for years, but about a year or so ago a new employee started working at the mailbox location. Bill seemed like a nice enough guy and was always helpful if I forgot the key to my mailbox or if I had a package.

A few times, though, he made sexual comments that if I wasn't paying close enough attention, I could have missed the true meaning of his remark and its intention. It seemed like he had practiced it since he was so sly with fitting the rude comment in with a compliment or another statement to mask the advance. There were times that even if I did catch the true meaning of the comment, I knew that he would deny it.

As you can imagine, this made me very uncomfortable, and I must admit I started to avoid going to my mailbox as often as I should because of it. I just did not want to deal with this guy unless I had to go in. There were times over about a three-month period that I felt like the Lord wanted to use me to speak to Bill about Jesus, but there was never the right moment.

One day, Bill said something that really made me angry because it was downright filthy. I left there feeling frustrated and didn't know how to respond to his rude comment. I called my mom and asked her how I should handle it the next time he made one of those sexual remarks.

She said, "Ashley, you simply tell him that you are a lady, and that you would appreciate it if he would not say those things." This seemed like something I could say back to him that would not be too argumentative, yet it was direct and to the point. She was right, and frankly, I was getting fed up with his rude comments.

The next day I decided I would drive over to my mailbox just because I was on a mission to call this guy out. Before I got there, God spoke to me and said, "Ashley, what are you doing? He's not even there today. When it is time, I will give you the right words to say. But, Ashley, only say what I would say to you, as I have words for him."

When I heard God say this, my pride sank in my spirit. There was this side of me that was ready to tell this guy like it is, and that he needed to be respectful to me. But I knew God was right. I did, however, still go in to check my mail box. And what do you know? He wasn't in that day. I chuckled because Bill was always there when I went in, and when I saw he wasn't there, I knew that voice was, indeed, God telling me to cool it.

The weekend came and went. In the middle of the next week, I drove my daughter to school. As I was driving, I passed the store where my mailbox is located. I heard the Lord speak to me in my spirit saying, "I want you to go to your mailbox today and speak to him but only say what I tell you."

Gladly, I did a U-turn and drove back to the store. I walked in, and there he was, standing behind the counter. I walked directly to my mailbox and there was nothing in it. So I said, "Well, no mail must be a good thing since that means no bills!"

He said, "Oh let me check the back for you since sometimes the postman can miss things." He walked back out and told me, "Nope. Looks like there's nothing for you today."

As I started to walk out the door I looked back and said, "I guess you can be a nice guy when you want to be."

He then looked at me with a sad face and said, "You mean this nice guy who is about to be fired?" That kind of shocked me so I asked why. He said with a sarcastic tone, "Two or three women have complained about me, saying that I was making sexual comments to them."

He was upset because these women reported him to his corporate office. He was irritated because he suggested that they were lying, like these ladies were somehow making this stuff up about him or something.

Oh, don't you know my blood started boiling? I wanted so bad to say what I wanted to say to him? This was the perfect moment for me to tell him he had done this to me, and that I knew he was lying. It reminded me of when Jesus confronted the Pharisees for lying, except I didn't have any compassion in my heart for this guy like Jesus did. Hey, I'm only human! But I still need to be obedient to God even though I knew Bill was lying. Truth be told, what I really wanted to say was, "Bill you are a lying devil, and you know it!" "You belong to your father, the devil, and you want to carry out your father's desires. He was a murderer from the beginning, not holding to the truth, for there is no truth in him. When he lies, he speaks his native language, for he is a liar and the father of lies" (John 8:44).

I heard God speak in my spirit "Don't say it, Ashley. Say what I would say *only!*" I knew I had to hold my tongue.

Bill went on and on about the accusations against him, and to tell you the truth, some of the things he said made me want to jump over the counter and wring his neck. In an effort to control my mouth, I just listened and prayed. In my thoughts, I said, "Lord, You are going to have to help me. Please give me the right words to say. I know this is not about me and what Bill has said or done. This is about what You want me to do to help Bill."

Then it came out of my mouth. To my surprise, I said, "Bill, do you know Jesus?" I felt my body go numb. I started thinking, "Where the heck did that come from?"

He stopped, looked at me, and then said, "Well, I'm Jewish."

So I told him, "Well, that's OK. Jesus was Jewish."

Then he dismissed me and started telling me all about how this was only his third job in his life, and that he used to work for a really big company in a highly paid position, and they did him wrong and owed him a lot of money. He continued to tell me that he was only doing this job to make his wife happy and to get out of the house.

If you want to know the truth, in this moment, all I could hear was him saying blah, blah, blah. He was boasting and then complaining about all that was wrong with the world, and to tell you the truth, it was driving me crazy. The excuses were absurd! I had my hand on the exit door ready to get the heck out of there. But suddenly I remembered something my dad said in a sermon about how to talk to people about eternity. I turned away from the door back toward Bill and said, "Bill, where will you be in one thousand years?"

He stopped his blabbering (thank God) and looked at me like I had two heads, which is funny because the next thing that came out of his mouth was about as strange as anything I have ever heard in my life. He said, waving his hands in the air, "I don't know! For all I know, in a thousand years, I will be a microorganism floating around in outer space somewhere!"

If you are anything like me, you must be thinking, "Wait! What?"

I thought, "Really? This guy is Jewish. He knows that's not true! His parents must have at least taught him about creation."

I laughed and said, "Bill, what happened to Adam when God created him and breathed into his nostrils?"

He thought about it for a second and said, "Well, he lived."

I said, "Yes, Adam became alive with the very breath of God." Then the next words of wisdom popped out of my mouth, "Bill, how long has God been around?"

Bill replied with his second crazy notion, "I don't know. For all I know God has tentacles!"

Oh man! This conversation just kept getting better and better. I thought to myself as I was speaking to God in my spirit, "How in the world can I have a comeback with this one, God?" Then it hit my mind, and I put my hand on my hip and gave him that look. You know the one I'm talking about. The look that says, "Come on, dude! You have got to be crazy now."

The next words plopped out of my mouth so quickly. "Didn't the Bible say that God made us in His image, Bill? So if we were made in His image, then don't we look just like God? And if God breathed into Adam and God lives forever, then don't you think you will live forever somewhere when your body dies?"

He just looked at me in amazement with eyes as large as golf balls. I proceeded to speak since Bill was now speechless. "So Bill, I will ask you again. Where will you be in a thousand years? I don't care what you have done in your life and all the jobs you have had or about all the awards that you have received. When you die, none of that stuff will matter. What I care to know is where you will be when you die, Bill?"

He stopped and looked at me with tears in his eyes. "I don't know," he said.

Suddenly, I felt genuine compassion for this poor man. I said, "Please do me a favor and go read Isaiah 53 tonight. When you read it, figure out who Isaiah was talking about hundreds of years before Jesus died on the cross for you, Bill. It will be at that point that you need to get on your knees, ask God to forgive you, and ask Jesus to be your Lord. Will you do that for me, Bill?"

He said, "Yes, I will."

With my heart softened toward him, I said, "Bill, I have had this feeling in my spirit that the Lord has wanted me to talk to you about Jesus for a few months now, and here I stand in front of you just before you are about to get fired. That is no coincidence." Then the store door opened and customers walked in. I held out my hand to shake his and said, "Goodbye, Bill. I will come by tomorrow to see what you think of Isaiah 53."

The next day, I went back up to my mailbox, but he was not there. So I went back a few days later, and he was not there again. I assumed he did, indeed, get fired from his job.

I was proud of myself for following the promptings of the Holy Spirit through the entire conversation. To be straight with you, I really do feel better that I didn't say what I wanted to say in my flesh to Bill. It is much more gratifying to think this man got his life right with God than to have made him feel even more like a sinner. There is no freedom in sin and, let's face the facts, he was already condemned. I didn't need to add to his struggle.

My prayer for Bill is that he did go home and read Isaiah 53, and that it touched his heart. I pray that the veil of deception that blinded him from the truth was lifted from his eyes because of our conversation.

The prophet Isaiah said something so profound regarding the Jewish people in Isaiah 6:10, and John reaffirmed it like this: "He has blinded their eyes and hardened their hearts, so they can neither see with their eyes, nor understand with their hearts, nor turn—and I would heal them" (John 12:40).

I may not ever see Bill again on this earth. I was really hoping to see him turn to Jesus as his Lord and Savior. But it doesn't matter whether or not I know if he gave his heart to the Lord that day. What matters is I planted a seed in his heart that God made Bill in His image, and that God wants Bill to come into a right relationship with Him through the promised Messiah.

I do, however, hope to see Bill in heaven one day. If I do, I will know it was not me that got him there. It was God's love through me for this man that opened his eyes and showed him the love of Papa God.

Who knows, maybe in a thousand years, Bill and I can go sit on the rings of Saturn in outer space and laugh because of our conversation about him thinking he might be a microorganism floating around and that God had tentacles. Maybe I'll play a prank on him and show up at the pearly gates in an octopus costume when he enters heaven. Hey! It could happen, and I think it would be fun! That's not any more crazy than what Bill said about God having tentacles.

From this experience, I learned that no matter how uncomfortable I feel around someone and how sinful someone is, God still loves them. It's Papa God's heart to see them set free. I am grateful that God chose to use me that day, and I know He is pleased with my obedience to say only what the Holy Spirit would say. Don't be afraid to speak out and say the truth in love. The truth is what sets us free. I say "us" because I was set free that day, too. I learned not to judge people the way the world judges but to love and see people the way that God sees them.

I still get a good giggle from this testimony. I told God, "If You look like Squidward on Sponge Bob, then where are all my tentacles? I seriously could use a few more sets of hands." Ha! Ha! Ha!

Big hugs,
Papa God and Ashley

The Lion of Judah

The first time Jesus came to this earth, He came as a Lamb. The second time He comes, He's returning as a Lion. Church body, be watchful and careful that our version of God is not distorted. Yes, God is loving and full of compassion and mercy for His people, but He is still sitting on the throne as the Judge; the Lion of Judah.

In Old Testament days, God was considered a warrior, and that is why when Jesus came as a baby, it confused the Jewish people. Jesus came to show us His love for us through servanthood and to become a living sacrifice. The people of that time expected the Lion instead of a Lamb. They thought Jesus would be a king like David who would destroy the enemies who tormented and persecuted them. Instead, He unexpectedly came as an innocent baby in a manger and was born in Judea. (See Matt. 2:1.) "But you, Bethlehem Ephrathah, though you are small among the clans of Judah, out of you will come for me one who will be ruler over Israel, whose origins are from of old, from ancient times. Therefore Israel will be abandoned until the time when she who is in labor bears a son, and the rest of his brothers return to join the Israelites" (Mic. 5:2–3).

God fulfilled Micah's prophecy of Jesus, pinpointing the exact location of His birth. God's plans are not our plans, His ways are not our ways, yet He always has the best plan to destroy the plans of His enemy and save His people. He clearly tells us His plans through His prophets in the Old and New Testaments. He's not hiding what is to come or how He will accomplish His plan.

Now, in present day, people are desensitized by God's mercy and grace, taking advantage of His love, but they are forgetting or trying to do away with the past. We need to remember the God of the Old Testament.

I encourage you to read two books of the Old Testament: Habakkuk and Zephaniah. In the text, watch for patterns and see for yourself what is to come if we don't repent before God. To repent means to turn away from sin, not just asking for forgiveness and then continuing with the sin. Repentance is doing an about-face—turning away from, walking away, and never looking back. Scripture repeatedly tells us that there is and will be judgment for the condemned. Maybe the verdict isn't always right away, but it will come. They can't run or hide from it. It is coming if they don't repent. Even Christians will be held accountable for what we have or haven't done to advance the kingdom of God. "He rules the world in righteousness and judges the peoples with equity" (Ps. 9:8).

It doesn't take a rocket scientist to figure out that the world we live in is full of chaos and war. Even rumors of worldwide war are circulating fast. If we look at history, we see the patterns of destruction that came upon an unrepentant and unruly people. The past tells us a lot about our future. Evil never changes, and good never changes. It's almost like a repeat button is being pushed every few decades. People just keep going in a cycle of sin and then repentance, disobedience and then remorse, disrespect for God and then respect for God because of regret for wrongdoings when judgment finally comes.

It's been over two thousand years since Christ died as the Lamb and rose again for our sins as the Lion, conquering sin and death.

Are we still repeating the past and so blind to think that the king of Judah isn't returning? Even more alarming: Are we fooling ourselves to think that He is turning a blind eye to the sin happening all around us? If that were the case, then why would Jesus even come to earth as the sacrifice in the first place?

We know that God believes we are worth it, and that is why He did it. Let us not forget why He came and what He did on our behalf. God is the same yesterday, today, and forever. He never changes, and He never lies.

I believe that we are living in the final hours of the last days. When studying Scripture and prophecy and noting what is happening in our world today, it is apparent that Jesus is, indeed, coming back soon. Prophecy is playing out like a movie right before our very eyes. Will it be months or years from now? I don't know that answer, but I know that 1 Thessalonians 5:2–3 says He will come like a thief in the night, unexpected by those who are asleep and not paying attention. Notice that it says those who are asleep, not those who are awake. Hebrews 6:4–8 talks about the great falling away of the church that must happen before the return of Christ:

> It is impossible for those who have once been enlightened, who have tasted the heavenly gift, who have shared in the Holy Spirit, who have tasted the goodness of the word of God and the powers of the coming age and who have fallen away, to be brought back to repentance. To their loss they are crucifying the Son of God all over again and subjecting him to public disgrace. Land that drinks in the rain often falling on it and that produces a crop useful to those for whom it is farmed receives the blessing of God. But land that produces thorns and thistles is worthless and is in danger of being cursed. In the end it will be burned.

So the real question is, are we ready, and are we paying attention to the fulfillment of the Scriptures? Are we ready for the return of Jesus Christ? I think we can agree that a true revival of the church is in desperate need. Revival starts within us and pours out to others in need of reviving. Otherwise, the church is dead until it is hit by the power of the Holy Spirit. This reminds me of someone in the ER who has had a heart attack and the doctors use defibrillators to jump-start their heart to bring them back to life. The church needs to live again as in the book of Acts. The book of Acts is a book of action. It is still happening today, and its purpose is that we continue this story in our generation—to act like the people in the book of Acts.

Lately, the Holy Spirit has been urgently speaking to me about repentance, not only for myself, but for this nation. If Jesus were to come back tomorrow, I don't want to be found sleeping and living life without telling others that time is short. How about you? Are you ready for Jesus to return? We must tell others to repent now and show them the way out of the darkness into the light. "'The people dwelling in darkness have seen a great light, and for those dwelling in the region and shadow of death, on them, a light has dawned.' From that time Jesus began to preach, saying, 'Repent, for the kingdom of heaven is at hand'" (Matt. 4:16–17 ESV).

Time is short and there is much risk in keeping the message of Jesus and repentance to ourselves. Very lives and eternal lives are at stake. It's time for the church to stand up and say, "Not on my watch!"

The time as watchman is at an end. We can't keep waiting for something major to happen before we repent and surrender to God. It's a new season, and the clock is ticking down.

Because of sin, we live in a dark world, but God knew we needed a Savior and the solution to sin was and still is, Jesus, who came as a Lamb but is returning very soon as the Lion. God's plan going forward is to use you and me to be the hands and feet of Jesus.

If you realize that you have been sleeping and know it is time to wake up, take this moment to repent and ask God to help you. He will show you what you need to repent of. He will also show you to others who want to help and what to say to those who need to know the truth. Take refuge in the Lord that His words will prevail, and we are safe under the shadow of the Almighty. "The LORD roars from Zion, and utters his voice from Jerusalem, and the heavens and the earth quake. But the LORD is a refuge to his people, a stronghold to the people of Israel" (Joel 3:16 ESV).

Church, it's time to act because the King is coming no longer as a baby in the manger. He's coming as the Lion, and He is ready to roar! I will leave you with this thought. Are you ready to be a world changer? If so, make this declaration with me. "Papa God, let's change the world!"

Big hugs,
Papa God and Ashley

Total Enjoyment

A Poem by Bonita Sawyer

Papa, my Father God,
I want to see what You see.
I want to be who You have designed and destined me to be.
I want to be in Your presence.
I want Your abiding presence in me in humble adoration to You.
I want the Issachar anointing.
I want to touch You.
I want to love as You love . . . fill me.
I want to laugh as You laugh.
I want to cry at what makes You cry . . . by Your grace, strengthen me.
I want to smile as You smile.
I want to enjoy what You enjoy.
I want to be proud of what You are proud of.
I want to accept what You accept.
I want to expel what You expel.
I want to speak what You are saying.

I want to joke what You laugh about.

I want to have Your humor . . . the joy of the Lord.

I want to be bold and hate what You hate.

I want to make happen what You want to have done.

I want to be kind as You are kind.

I want to have healing flowing through me like You have flow through You.

In all this, I want to be close to You, Holy Spirit . . .

Help me to keep my hands clean and my heart pure.

Help me to see through the muck and mire of a person's life to get the redemption with hope and love of tenderness that can only come from You.

I want You to be proud of me.

I want to enjoy EVERY part of the journey with You.

I want You, Holy Spirit, to be my BEST FRIEND.

I want to see, hear, act in response to Your voice without hesitation (maybe pause to discern) by Your grace and anointing, to do Your will on earth as it is in heaven.

From You, ADONAI, I want to know the purpose and plan for my life . . . so I will look for You in the "set-ups" for my life with You.

I want the twins, Faith and Trust, to be in operation in me. Oh Lord, that Your Light will always be on me, as I stay close to You and always with a humble, gracious, giving, and receiving heart.

For Your Honor and Glory, and for me to enjoy You in the process.

Oh, yeah, I want a big, beautiful, well-oiled brain, filled with all kinds of capabilities for You, my Papa.

Thank you,

Your daughter/son, Your Favorite One[8]

---

8   used by permission

Author Contact

10006 Cross Creek Blvd. #401
Tampa, FL 33647

Website

www.papagodandashley.com

Order Information

To order additional copies of this book, please visit
www.redemption-press.com.
Also available on Amazon.com and BarnesandNoble.com
Or by calling toll free 1-844-2REDEEM.

CPSIA information can be obtained
at www.ICGtesting.com
Printed in the USA
FFOW05n0825060917